Restoring and Renovating
Antique Furniture

Restoring and Renovating Antique Furniture

TOM ROWLAND

with drawings by Ronald Reeves

William Luscombe

First published in Great Britain by
WILLIAM LUSCOMBE PUBLISHER LTD
The Mitchell Beazley Group
Artists House
14, Manette Street
London W1V 5LB
1976

ISBN 0 86002 085 1

Text set in 11/12 pt. Photon Baskerville, printed
by photolithography,
and bound in Great Britain at The Pitman Press,
Bath

Contents

Illustrations

Preface

GIVING YOU CONFIDENCE

Before jumping straight into the techniques of the restoration and renovation of antique furniture it seems sensible to pause for a moment and consider what kind of furniture you are going to restore. You have, no doubt, in the back of your mind, several things around the house that have been nagging away as tasks to be done, but if these involve prized and valuable pieces of furniture you are rightly hesitant about practising on *them*.

First of all, you will want to gain confidence and experience and the only way to do that is to practise. The object of this book is to acquaint you with the well-tried and widely used techniques which the professional restorer employs; I will, I hope, instil a feeling of confidence, because the techniques of restoration are not particularly difficult to master. The one thing that you will have to do for yourself entirely is to practise in order to make perfect.

You need not be frightened. Short of taking a chopper to a piece of furniture it is difficult to damage it beyond repair. If you do make mistakes, they can be rectified with no more than the consumption of your time and the attendant frustrations that go with having to do a job twice or three times. If initially you find your confidence flagging remember the old Chinese proverb 'The longest of journeys starts with a single step'. The most difficult to take is always the first step, but once embarked on the journey the remainder becomes increasingly easier and at the same time increasingly rewarding and entertaining.

The one salient mistake that the 'amateur' is inclined to make is that of giving up too soon. Ninety five per cent of any job is the preparatory work. The full reward of seeing the job start to pull itself together only comes in the last stages, sometimes in the last few minutes. It is very easy to get discouraged, to think you have not succeeded during the preparatory part of the work and to finish off in a slapdash manner, when all that is needed is a few more minutes work.

Always remember, particularly while you are gaining your confidence through practice, to retain, if you can, the virtue of patience.

So where do you start? Obviously not in the antique shops, for here most of the things displayed for sale are in near perfect condition, ready to be put into immediate use by the proud purchaser. The back street junk shops and street market are fertile stamping grounds which can provide you with suitable bits for resurrection, but best of all, providing you have the necessary courage to approach your friends, neighbours and even complete strangers, are lofts, garden sheds, farmers barns, cellars and all the places where unwanted things have been tucked away and forgotten.

Fashions change and memories are short. A few years ago Victorian and Edwardian furniture by the ton was discarded, as being old-fashioned and out of date. It was pushed into the spare room or the outhouse to make way for new and stylish furniture. Today Victorian furniture is at a premium and rising in value more rapidly than any other style of 'antique'. Even the Art Deco furniture of the nineteen twenties and thirties is enjoying a vogue of popularity. The kind of things that you want to look for fall into three rough categories.

(a) Those things that are of practical use, such as tables, chairs, chests of drawers, sideboards, desks, china cupboards, stools and the like;

(b) Those things that are suitable for converting into something else, like bedroom commodes which can be turned into bedside tables, needlework boxes, coffee tables, or sometimes miniature chests of drawers. Wash-hand stands which will convert into writing tables, dressing tables or sideboards; and

(c) interesting ornaments such as clocks, candlesticks, small boxes, tea caddies, writing boxes, gramophone cabinets, carvings, old tools and kitchen utensils; in fact anything of general interest which will become a talking point or a decorative feature after it has been cleaned, repaired and repolished.

Never turn down any piece of furniture, particularly if it is made of mahogany, walnut, oak or rosewood. One of your most valuable acquisitions will be a stock of various woods to be used for repairs to other things which you find, that are suitable for rescuing. Old veneers can be soaked off pieces of furniture and used for patching, for old veneers are usually thicker than modern ones and will match in better, requiring less preparation work before polishing and finishing. Old leaves from tables and sides of wardrobes provide you with a stock of good raw material, well-seasoned and far cheaper than wood purchased from a timber merchant. Indeed, today you may have great difficulty in finding a woodyard that sells English oak, South American mahogany, any kind of walnut, elm, or fruitwoods. Most of their stocks consist, apart from softwoods, of Japanese oak, African mahoganies, and beech.

If you are really stuck, beech is the best wood to fall back on; it can be stained up to resemble any wood. It is hard, but easily worked and polished and, above all, it is universally available.

Most people want pieces of furniture to use, not to stand in a corner to be admired. So when purchasing pieces of furniture to restore, your first thought must be for something that is going to be either useful or at least decorative and pleasing to the eye. Much mid and late Victorian furniture is 'fussy', with too much carving and twiddly bits, fretwork mouldings and turned wooden knobs. These should not put you off, as they can, more often than not, be removed. Even ugly carved door panels can be taken out of their frames and reversed to show the plain inside surface. Turned wooden feet on chests-of-drawers are easily removed and replaced with bracket feet similar to those of the Eighteenth Century. Turned wooden handles can be replaced with reproduction brass ones (a large range is available from specialist suppliers). In other words, a little alteration to the decoration of an ugly piece of furniture can obliterate or remove the offensive elements and turn it into an acceptable, even a beautiful piece by modern standards.

Bad colour should not discourage you either. Remember that our Victorian ancestors liked their mahogany furniture heavy, rich purple in colour and French polished so highly that the surfaces resembled sheets of glass. Most wood is not naturally this, now unfashionable colour; the finish is usually artificial and can be removed without too much effort, revealing the natural beauty of the wood. Even Eighteenth Century furniture was often repolished to suit current Victorian fashion and similarly this can be restored to its original glorious condition.

Most exciting of all, painted furniture is not always plain pine underneath the layers of brown, white, cream and green paint. A little judicious scraping in an unobtrusive place with a pen-knife may reveal mahogany or walnut. If you are lucky it may even have cross banding and inlay.

Even pine furniture is not to be dismissed lightly. Stripped pine pieces can be very beautiful and from time to time enjoy great popularity. Really good pine furniture has always been sought after, particularly if it has a little bit of carving on it. Look out for corner cupboards, small tables and dressers particularly. They are always desirable acquisitions.

Perhaps most rewarding of all are pieces of furniture that no longer have a use in modern homes.

Now we live in smaller, easier to heat, houses, the huge pieces of furniture favoured by our ancestors are not much use to us. Chests-of-drawers are often far too high to fit beneath our large picture windows, and can be purchased relatively cheaply. They can be cut down by removing the bottom (or sometimes the top) drawer. Girls no longer require bottom drawers—so the best thing to do is to dispense with them. You need to develop an eye for proportion. These chests of drawers are often very large and you must visualise what they will look like when reduced in height by one drawer. The result is, more often than not, pleasing, but you can get caught out if you fail to picture it in your mind's eye as it will be *after* you have altered it.

Considerable numbers of bedroom commodes are still to be found in junk shops and auction rooms. They come in a variety of designs, two of which are ideal for alteration into delightful and useful pieces of furniture for your home. The first is the lift up top variety which resembles a miniature chest of drawers, usually four drawers high. These can be turned into what they were built to resemble by removing the insides and building drawers on to the false fronts and fixing runners into the sides of the carcase. The second variety, are variations of square boxes on legs, again with fitted interiors. These can be de-gutted and turned into needlework boxes, bedside tables or cocktail cabinets.

George III mahogany commode with a lift up top: suitable for conversion into miniature chest of drawers

Georgian step commode. Converts easily into telephone stool or library steps

Victorian mahogany commode. Converts into needlework box, storage chest—fireside stool (Fit bracket feet)

Less attractive, but equally adaptable are what is known as step commodes. These convert into telephone tables, work boxes or library steps. The steps themselves are often covered with old pieces of carpet. If these are removed and replaced with tooled leather the effect is very pleasing.

Next you should keep an eye open for wardrobes. These do not usually convert immediately into useful furniture, but they have the great advantage of being a cheap source of excellent seasoned wood. They are cheap, because few people want wardrobes today. Most houses have built in wardrobes and in consequence sale rooms have difficulty in obtaining a bid for these bulky pieces of bedroom furniture. They can often be purchased for less than you would have to pay for their hinges, handles, locks, screws and mirror, were you to buy them at current prices in an ironmongers. These fittings are almost invariably made of brass and, of course, can be used again. The wood used for the construction consists of large pieces and long lengths. If you spend a little time in taking them to pieces carefully, you have materials for the construction of coffee-tables, hanging or standing shelves, trays, bedside-tables and cupboards, picture frames and, above all, spare wood for repairing other pieces of furniture, such as making bracket feet to replace turned ones on Victorian chests of drawers.

Old wash-stands should be studied with imagination. Usually they have a tiled back; often a marble top. The oblong ones are easily adaptable into serving-tables, writing-tables, dressing-tables and, of course, the corner wash-stands make marvellous settings for plant and flower arrangements, or shelves for displaying glass and china.

These, of course, are only the more obvious examples of the ways in which no longer acceptable furniture can be transformed. Do not think that there is anything wrong with these adaptations. Once your eyes are opened to the possibilities, you will be able to spot examples of these conversions in many antique shops, and will be surprised at how much money they fetch. So, apart from just buying up antiques in bad condition and renovating them, you can have hours of pleasure in converting old and no longer useful pieces into attractive and delightful furnishings for your home.

Chapter 1

THE TOOLS OF THE TRADE

The fortunate restorer has a garden shed, a garage or a spare room which he can devote entirely to his hobby. If you are going to be successful and enjoy to the full your labours it is essential to have somewhere to set aside the work in progress while the glue dries or the polish hardens. Somewhere that you can leave things undisturbed, without all the fag of getting everything out each time you have an hour, or even a few minutes, to spare.

The space you require need not necessarily be large: many a professional restorer works in a sectional garden shed or an old outhouse.

Most handymen and women have a collection of tools, among them some old, inherited ones. In restoration work old tools are of great value, for the problems to be solved are often different from those of the cabinet maker and joiner. Many awkward and irregular joints have to be made so a wide variety of cramps and securing devices are required. Old, rusted nails and stubborn screws have to be removed. Irregular shapes have to be fashioned to replace broken or lost parts. Broken beadings of a pattern no longer available from timber merchants have to be fabricated.

For these jobs you will often use old tools which would normally have been discarded as past all practical use. Many of the tools you will want are not commercially available and you will have to make them, and for doing this, old tools can often be adapted. But first of all let us examine the standard equipment that you should acquire. There is one golden rule when buying tools. Only buy the best, they are the cheapest in the end. Perhaps you know the story of the pedlar who was selling razors in the market place. Someone bought one, tried to use it, found it useless and returned it to the hawker before he had left the market.

"What on earth use is a razor whose blade will not hold an edge" the man asked. "You see" replied the pedlar, "These razors are not meant for shaving with, they are so cheap, they are only meant for selling".

There are unfortunately a lot of tools around that, like the pedlar's razors, are only meant for selling. They are made of cheap steel, badly designed and awkward to hold. They become unusable within a very short time and cause untold frustration.

On the other hand good tools can last not one, but several lifetimes. I have some tools, still in daily use, that are over 150 years old.

In order to simplify this list we will divide it up into stages that a piece of furniture may have to go through before it emerges from the workshop in its newly resurrected state.

1. *Cleaning and Stripping*
Only a few tools are required for these operations:—
Coarse and Fine steel wool (Grade 3 or 4 and grade 00 or 000). Good quality *pliable* chisel scrapers—the kind you use for stripping wallpaper and a narrower one with a blade about 1½ inches. A selection of 'scrubbing' brushes (old tooth brushes, boot brushes, nail brushes, etc.).

The other materials will be discussed later on in the book.

2. *Cabinet-making and Woodworking Tools*
The first essential is a good solid bench fitted with at least one reliable woodworking vice, a bench stop and, if possible, a bench holdfast.

As far as hand tools are concerned, the following list constitutes a working, though not exhaustive, selection of desirable tools. It stands to reason that few of you will buy all of these tools at once. Many of them you will have already. It is far better to acquire your additional tools gradually. The absolutely essential tools are printed in capitals.

Saws

Rip Saw	(cutting with grain)	4 points to inch
PANEL SAW	(cutting across wood)	10 points to inch
TENON SAW	(cutting joints)	14–16 points to inch
GENTS HACK SAW	(small cuts)	20–32 points to inch
Coping Saw	(cutting curves and holes)	
Padsaw	Fretsaw	

Hammers

CLAW HAMMER	16–20 OZ.
Cross Pein hammer	8–10 OZ.
TACK HAMMER or PIN HAMMER	
Pin Push	3/32" punch
Set of punches	

Planes

Joiners Plane	Block Plane
Jack Plane	Shoulder Plane
SMOOTH PLANE	Combination Plane

Chisels

BEVEL EDGE CHISELS	$\frac{1}{4}''$ $\frac{1}{2}''$ $\frac{3}{4}''$ $1''$
Firmer Gouge	$\frac{1}{2}''$ $1''$
Mortice Chisel	
OILSTONE (INDIA) FINE OR MEDIUM	
HONING GUIDE	
Spokeshave	
STANLEY KNIFE	

Rasps

Flat Surform
Small Surform
10" HALFROUND RASP
Cylindrical Rasp
Cabinet Scraper
Two rifflers   SANDPAPER BLOCK

Screwdrivers

Heavy Screwdriver	20"
Medium Screwdriver (London pattern)	14"
SMALL Screwdriver	6"
MIDGET	3"
Awl — BRADAWL	

WHEEL BRACE
SET TWIST DRILLS   COUNTERSINK BIT
TRY SQUARE
Marking Gauge   Mortice Gauge
STRAIGHT EDGE   RULE 2 ft.   10 ft. TAPE
6 G CRAMPS   2 SASH CRAMPS
Pliers   Pincers
2 CHISEL SCRAPERS $1\frac{1}{2}$" & $2\frac{1}{2}$"

Power Tools

Two speed drill	Circular saw attachment and table
Burgess Bandsaw	Grindstone
Lathe attachment	Face Grinder

3. *Finishing, Colouring and Polishing*

Very few 'tools' as such are required for these operations. They consist only of a range of brushes, rags and dusters. Cotton wool is required for the application of stains and making up French polishing rubbers. Various grades of sand or garnett paper are also used.

Care of Tools

Having acquired a kit of tools, they should be looked after properly. They should not be tumbled together in a box or drawer and left in the humid atmosphere of a garage or shed. If this practice is followed, the edge tools such as chisels will be chipped and blunted. Rust will attack the steel, the handles will be damaged by sharp edges and general rapid deterioration will quickly result.

It is best, where possible, to keep tools in a rack behind the work-bench. They should be wiped over fairly regularly with a rag impregnated with light machine oil.

Sets of carving chisels, turning chisels and other tools only occasionally used, should be stored in a tool roll. Saw blades should be protected with either a plastic or a wood lath cover to prevent damage to the points of the blade.

Some tradesmen favour a fitted tool chest in which every tool has its own place and is held in place in such a way that it cannot damage, or be damaged, by other tools.

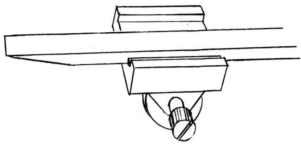

'Eclipse' Honing Gauge

You should also cultivate workshop discipline and replace each tool in its place in the tool rack before using the next one required. It takes a lot of willpower to follow this practice, but nothing is more frustrating than having to search around for a tool that has been carelessly laid aside and temporarily lost. Learning to replace tools in their own place after use saves hours of wasted time searching for them.

Keeping tools sharp is often the most difficult task to be faced by the 'amateur' craftsman. I know one person who has a large selection of chisels—all blunt. He goes out to buy a new sharp one every time he has a job to do! While this is going to extreme ends to own a sharp tool, it is easy to sympathise, for you have to learn the technique of sharpening edge tools and understand the mechanics of this process. Both plane blades and chisels are sharpened in the same way, and should have two angles making up their cutting edge: a ground angle at $25°$ and a honed angle at $30°$. While experienced craftsmen can judge these angles by eye, until you are skilled it is as well to use an Eclipse Honing Gauge This cheap little tool makes the task of sharpening both chisels and planes a simple operation.

For sharpening, you need a good, *flat* oilstone. A combination stone with medium grit on one side and fine grit on the other is best, and either carborundum or India stone is suitable. These should be moistened with a few drops of light machine oil each time before use. The 25° angle is ground in on a coarse or medium stone. The 30° cutting edge is ground on a fine stone and will be observed as a 'line of light' when

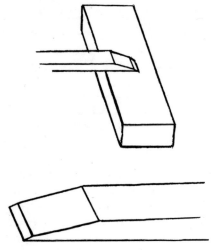

Hone the sloping side (to 30°), then the flat side (above) to remove the wire edge

correctly ground. When you have sharpened the tool, you will feel a burr on the flat side by running your thumb along the back of the blade. This is removed by rubbing the flat side on the stone, taking great care to ensure that it is held absolutely flat on stone otherwise the razor edge will be blunted. If the burr does not come off at once, alternative honing of the edge and rubbing of the back will reduce the joint of the burr until it falls off.

Good quality tools which are properly tempered by the manufacturer will hold a sharp edge for a good time, but when working on hard woods, rehoning as soon as the edge becomes dull should be done frequently. Only the 30° angle has to be honed. When the 'line of light' becomes broad, regrinding at 25° is necessary. If you have a grindstone this

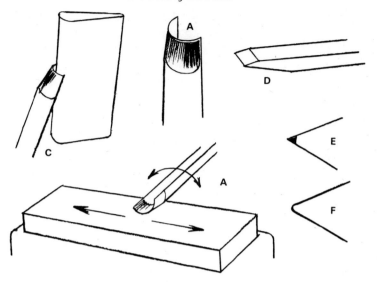

When sharpening gouges, rotate on India or Carborundum stone A and look for line of light B. The inner bevel is sharpened with a shaped India stone C. Both angles at about 15° D.
With a parting tool sharpen the angle E to a "U" shape to aid cutting F. Sharpen each angle separately on stone on both outer and inner surfaces

saves a lot of time, but it is not essential as the medium or coarse stone can be used to do this.

Always remember, a blunt tool is a more dangerous tool than a sharp one. You have to apply more pressure to it and it can easily slip!

A different technique is required for sharpening gouges and carving tools and for this you require in addition a set of shaped slip stones. These are held in the hand, unlike your oilstone, which should be secured to the bench.

When carving tools and gouges are bought, they are ground to an angle of about 15°. It is common practice to hone both the inner and outer edges to about 15° bevels. The outer edges of curved gouges are honed on a fine oilstone, running the bevel at right angles down the stone, rotating it gently at the same time. Care should be taken not to round the two corners of the blade.

The inner surface is ground with a lightly oiled slipstone with a suitably rounded cutting face. The burr, if any, is removed and the sharpening completed by stropping on a piece of soft leather dressed with Crocus powder and oil.

The reason for the inner bevel on a gouge is that, firstly it reduces friction while a cut is being made; secondly, when being used hollow side down, the tool can be lifted to make it easier to hold, and thirdly, a 30° bevel is more durable and will not crumble as quickly as a 15° bevel which is too thin for working on hard woods.

Carving chisels, which may have either a square or a skew (angled) blade are similarly sharpened on both sides, using an oilstone.

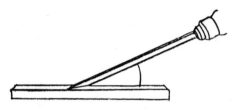

Final stroppings of carving tools on leather pad, dressed with oil and crocus powder

Parting tools are best sharpened as gouges, but the V at the bottom point of the tool is slightly rounded into a U with the slipstone, as it is here that the first cut is made and it needs to be sharpest at this point. It is almost impossible to get a sharp angle at the point of these tools and, from a practical point of view, quite unnecessary.

Saws are made with varying numbers of teeth to the inch. The more points to the inch, the finer the cut. A 16 point saw cuts more finely, and more slowly, than one with 10 points to the inch.

Almost all saws have alternative points bent out in opposite directions. This is known as set and allows the saw to pass more easily through the wood, at the same time throwing out the sawdust and preventing the blades becoming clogged.

Saw blades do not dull as quickly as do those of edge tools, but should be sharpened and set from time to time. These days most good ironmongers have an arrangement with a professional saw doctor, and will undertake the sharpening for you. This is easier and better than attempting this job yourself.

SPECIAL TOOLS FOR THE RESTORER

In order to make the specialist work of restoration easier, you need to acquire or make a number of special tools.

Of prime importance is a range of cramps, many of which you can improvise. Firstly you need to buy at least half a dozen G cramps and a couple of sash cramps. In addition, you require a supply of transparent self-adhesive tape and self-adhesive masking tape, such as is used by coachbuilders to protect chrome parts on a motor-car when spray painting. These tapes are invaluable for holding small patches of wood in place while the glue is drying.

Upholstery springs, cut up into convenient hoops are valuable for holding awkward and irregular shapes, as are spring clothes pegs.

Lengths of clothes-line can be used as tourniquets and rubber bands are useful when holding smaller joints to set.

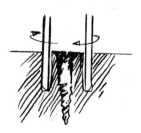

Special home-made tool for extracting rusted-in screws

A tool that you will have to make for the fabrication of small mouldings and cutting reeded edges on to tables etc. is a scratch stock. This tool is similar to a spokeshave, but instead of a cutting blade, it has a series of scratching blades, and has a stop incorporated to guide the tool along the straight edge of the wood being worked on. This tool should take only an hour or so to make from a piece of beech or mahogany. The shaping irons are held in place by a block of wood secured to the stock by two bolts fitted with thumb screws. The irons are made from pieces of an old saw blade or a tempered steel ruler. The profile of the shapes that they scratch out are filed into the metal with a set of warding and key cutting files. With this tool, surprisingly, you can shape ten or twelve foot of moulding in less than an hour.

You also want a collection of tools for removing old nails and rusted in screws. To prevent the slot of the screw from burring over, the blade of the screwdriver should be as tight a fit as possible, so you will require a selection. If a screw will not budge, first give the screwdriver head a few smart taps with a carpenter's hammer or mallet. If this does not loosen the screw, heat the head up with either a blow lamp, or if this will damage the surface of the surrounding wood, a soldering iron heated to cherry red. This will expand the screw, and as it cools down, loosen it from the surrounding wood. If this fails, you will have to drill it out.

For this you can make yourself some hollow drills using various diameter steel or bronze tubes, about 3 to 4 inches long. One end is serrated like the teeth of a saw with a triangular file. The other end is riveted or welded on to the shank of an old twist drill bit. This tool can be placed over the head of the screw, and a cylindrical hole drilled with it, using a brace. The core containing the screw can be removed and the hole plugged with matching wood.

A couple of padded resting boards are also desirable for resting polished surfaces on the floor or bench. These are 4" or 5" boards, about 3' 6" long, covered with baize or other soft material to protect polished surfaces from scratches.

This is by no means an exhaustive list. You will undoubtedly invent many other tools and devices as you progress. It is always worthwhile having a little 'think' about how any job can be done most easily, and building a special jig or tool to hold the work is often a great time saver.

Chapter 2

CLEANING, REVIVING AND STRIPPING

When you come to think of it both motor-cars and furniture have many things in common. They both need to be maintained as both suffer from neglect, sometimes to the extent that they cease to function efficiently. Both need polishing—the outside surfaces need the protection of wax. The working parts need oiling and greasing; for example, hinges, locks and drawer runners. Both require protection from the elements; furniture, particularly, from central heating which is an artificial 'element' only inflicted on furniture during the last quarter century.

From time to time both need running repairs as they are subject to fair wear and tear, and accidental bumps and scratches. When they are old and venerable they sometimes require complete rebuilding.

With antique furniture, particularly with good antique furniture, great integrity is called for. It may be quicker and easier to replace rather than to repair and preserve a worm-eaten leg of a 200 year-old chair, but replacement will reduce the value by as much as half, while repair will greatly increase the value while at the same time preserving authenticity. This integrity is required not only with repairs but also with the maintenance of the exterior—in other words, the cleaning and polishing. Before interfering with the surface of any piece of furniture, you must make certain that damage is not done to the combination of fading, polishing and handling over a period of many years, which gives a good antique the delightful mellowness and depth of colour and polish which is known as 'Patina'. Patina is possibly one of the most difficult things to define. As soon as you see it on an old piece of furniture you instantly recognise it. It is the finish created by time, light, care and attention, waxing and rubbing. The surfaces will have light areas where handling has been greatest and polishing easiest. Nooks, crannies and mouldings, and the less accessible areas will be darker with a combination of dirt or the original stain. It is not a particularly smooth or highly polished finish. Most of the original varnish and colour will have long since faded or have been rubbed off. It is a complete, delightful picture giving an impression of age and mellowness which defies imitation.

Of course, Patina does not exist on many pieces of furniture, particularly those that have been ill-treated and banished to the woodshed. The kinds of antique furniture that you are going to find for restoring are not those that have been well kept and maintained throughout their life-times and will have, most likely, descended from the Great House to the servants' quarters, from the servants' quarters to the gardener's cottage, from the gardener's cottage to the henhouse, and during this descent in status will have lost much, if not all, of their original lustre. But on rare occasion Parina may have been preserved beneath coats of paint applied at some time in the past when an attempt has been made to 'brighten it up a little bit'.

The first rule is, therefore, before sloshing stripper all over a newly acquired treasure, a little bit of judicious examination of what is underneath all the dirt, grime and paint is prudent. A test on an unobtrusive part of the article is called for to find out what lies beneath the surface, and here it is worthwhile examining the types of finish that have been used on furniture.

Almost all the surviving furniture before the reign of the Stewarts is of oak. During the Tudor period, furniture was undoubtedly made of other domestic timbers but such woods as elm, fruitwoods, beech and sycamore did not have the durability of oak, so in the main it is furniture built of this wood that survives. More often than not, if it has been polished at all, oak furniture has been polished with beeswax, and a pure wax polish of many years standing is the most beautiful.

From the time of the Restoration of Charles II to the throne, right the way into the reign of George I—1660–1730—walnut became the fashionable wood. That a great deal of this furniture still survives as it was manufactured is in great part due to the fact that so much of the earlier furniture was destroyed during the Fire of London, to be replaced by the newer and more fashionable walnut. The fashion quickly spread from the capital to the provinces. During this period polishing with linseed oil began to supersede the use of beeswax.

Towards the end of the reign of George I right through to the end of the reign of George III in 1820, South American and Cuban mahogany became the popular and fashionable wood for furniture construction. The eighteenth century was the golden age of English furniture making, during which time most of the great masters of furniture design were living. The Chippendales, Sheraton, Hepplewhite, Robert Adam and Thomas Hope are the leading exponents of eighteenth century English furniture design.

The standard method of polishing furniture at this time was to impregnate it with linseed oil and, after it had soaked in to the wood, burnish the surface with fine brick dust on a cork rubber.

Towards the end of the eighteenth century varnish finishing was extensively used, where resins were incorporated into the linseed oil in order to reduce the amount of labour required to achieve the final polish.

French polishing was not introduced into England until about 1820. This technique involves the application of a solution of a resin called Shelac dissolved in methylated spirit, with a pad made of cotton wool wrapped in a soft cloth.

You must remember, however, that the renovation of furniture is not a new art; it has been going on almost ever since furniture was invented and at some time or other most furniture has been renovated. Our Victorian ancestors, who loved highly polished and shiny things, French-polished nearly all the furniture they could lay their hands on, and at the same time incorporated into the finish a purply-red colour which was at that time the vogue. It is not unusual to come across pieces of furniture that have the original oil or varnish finish on the sides and a French-polished top.

From about the time of the Great War cellulose and other synthetic finishes were introduced.

When tackling the cleaning of a piece of furniture, therefore, it is as well to go through a number of stages before resorting to complete stripping. The first stage is to clean the piece of furniture down with soap and warm water. This will remove a great deal of the surface dirt and allow you to examine more closely the condition of the wood. Slightly more drastic is to clean down with white spirit (Turps substitute) and fine wire wool. Underneath you may find remnants of perished and crazed French polish or varnish. Crazed or perished surfaces can sometimes be revived using a variety of reviving agents. A number of proprietory products are available, amongst them 'Ringway', Furniglass No. 2 and McKeowns Restoration Cream, but other home-made revivers may also be effective. With all of them, however, a considerable amount of rubbing and polishing is required. The following mixtures are useful in this connection:

REVIVING SOLUTION

Butyr of Antimony	3 parts
Real Turpentine	3 parts
Malt Vinegar	10 parts
Methylated Spirits	10 parts
Raw Linseed Oil	13 parts

If you cannot get any Butyr of Antimony—few chemists shops have it these days, although specialist shops still keep it—a simpler reviver as follows can be made up:

Real Turpentine	2 parts
Linseed Oil	2 parts
Methylated Spirit	5 parts

The technique is to work over the surface with a soft pad of cotton material, using a circular motion. This will soften the surface and allow it to flow slightly, thus filling up the cracks and crazing.

Revivers are also effective in some cases for the removal of rings and stains caused by spilled drinks, flower vases, etc. You will only find them effective, however, if the damage is relatively superficial. If the alcohol or watermark has penetrated the polished surface it is usually quicker and more effective to strip the whole surface and re-polish it.

If you have decided that the original finish is so much deteriorated that it is not worth preserving, a good stripper should be used and, in eight cases out of ten, this is usually the most sensible thing to do. The technique of using a paint stripper is important to acquire if you are going to be successful and save yourself a great deal of unnecessary hard work.

First of all, choose the right paint stripper. My experience has been that Nitromors, which is easily available in most hardware and ironmongers shops, is the most effective. This comes in two grades, in a yellow tin designed for paint and polish stripping, and in a green tin which will also strip the new synthetic paints based on modern plastics. There is no need to use the latter stripper unless fairly recently painted surfaces have to be tackled, but either is equally effective on all furniture. Another good stripper is Perfecta which is only obtainable from Gedge & Co. of 88 St John Street, Clerkenwell, London E.C.1.

The technique is to flood the surface with the liquid, using a paint brush to spread it. You have to remember that you are not painting the stripper on to the surface but using sufficient to lift and soften the old polish or paint. Sometimes the old finish will start to peel off in a few seconds; sometimes it will have to soak for ten or fifteen minutes but, at all events, do not allow the surface to dry off. Where thick paint or polish is present, drying can be quite rapid as the stripper incorporates itself with the old finishing material, so keep on applying more and more stripper.

When the finish has lifted it can be scraped off carefully with a chisel scraper. Sometimes several repeated applications are required to remove successive layers. In most cases it is easier to scrape the remnants of the old finish over the edge of a piece of furniture on to a pad of old newspaper, otherwise you can make the most terrible mess.

When nearly all of the old polish has been removed, make a final application of the stripper and this time scrub it off with coarse wire wool. Great care must be taken to ensure that the last remnants of the old polish are removed and when scrubbing with wire wool, scrub in the same direction as the grain to prevent surface scratching. Grade 3 or 4 wire wool, the coarsest available, is the most suitable to use, although finer grades can be employed on more delicate woods, such as satinwood. Paint strippers can be used with safety on veneered furniture without danger of lifting the veneers. When the piece of furniture has been completely stripped and the last vestiges of the old finishes removed from the cracks and corners, the remaining stripper must be 'killed' by wiping over the entire surface with turpentine substitute. The piece of furniture should now be left to dry off.

Paint stripper, as well as removing old polishes, will often remove a certain amount of the original stain used to colour the wood and some surface stains caused by carelessness. Some persistent stains, particularly ink stains, often remain. Most people prefer to remove these if possible. In order to do this you have to employ a bleach, the most effective of these being a solution of oxalic acid in warm water. This white crystalline substance can be purchased from most chemists shops and is dissolved in warm water at the proportion of a heaped tablespoon to about a quart of water. It is most effective when used hot and again should be scrubbed into the stained areas with wire wool. The whole surface should be treated, however, otherwise there is a danger of producing a light area in the place which was previously stained.

Other bleaching materials can also be used. Hydrogen peroxide is sometimes effective; for more persistent stains an application of household ammonia on to the top of an application of Hydrogen Peroxide accelerates the bleaching process and sometimes the use of household bleaches will be successful in the removal of stains.

Chapter 3

GLUES AND GLUEING

The one thing that seems to frighten most people is the use of adhesives in furniture repairs, so you should read this chapter very thoroughly. If you follow the instructions carefully, you should have no more problems with glueing things together.

First of all, you must appreciate that, with very few exceptions, no other jointing device but glue is required to effect a secure repair. Engineers in particular, it would appear, distrust the strength of glue joints. I have on occasion removed from a previously repaired piece of furniture, particularly chairs, a collection of steel brackets, threaded rods, bolts, washers, plates and specially fashioned supports that is staggering in volume. All used because of a lack of trust in glue joints.

In order to make an effective glue joint you must observe a few simple rules.

Number One

The surfaces to be glued together must be absolutely clean and free from old glue, oil, grease or dust. Most old furniture was stuck together with glue made from animal hooves and horns, known variously as Animal Glue or Scotch Glue. It is a very good adhesive that has stood the test of time, but its main defects are that it is not resistant to moisture or damp and, when it gets too old and very dry, it tends to crystallise and perish—the latter only happens over a very long period, but can cause joint failures in chairs and other furniture joints subjected to repeated stress.

Old Scotch Glue can be cleaned off fairly easily by a combination of rasping or scraping off the thick areas and then scrubbing with warm water and a stiff brush to remove the thin residues. The joints must then be allowed to dry thoroughly before reglueing is attempted. Where loose joints that will not come apart easily are encountered, the joint should be irrigated with methylated spirit. This causes almost instant crystallisation of the glue and breaks the remains of the joint, which can then be tapped apart with a mallet. If a block of soft wood is placed on the polished surface of the part to be separated, and this, rather than the part, is struck with the mallet, no bruising or other damage will result while knocking the joint apart.

You may come across badly made or broken joints previously repaired with modern adhesives which are plastic or epoxy resin based. These residues are more difficult to remove, but, apart from rasping or sandpapering off, they can often be softened and removed with solvents, such as Acetone, Amyl acetate, cellulose thinners, and most effective a proprietory solvent called Disolvex which has recently come on to the market in retail packs.

Number Two

You cannot glue fresh air. In other words, the two surfaces to be fixed together must be in close contact with each other. You cannot use glues as a filler to bridge the gaps in loose joints. Very few glues have any strength on their own, so you must make the joints tight before glueing them. In some, such as sloppy mortice and tennon joints, a piece of thin veneer glue coated on both sides can be slipped into the mortice. In some cases both surfaces of the wood must be planned down to ensure uniform contact. With a new break, no matter how jagged, if it is glue back together again before damage is done to the edges, it can be made as good as new and almost completely invisible.

Number Three

You cannot glue end grain to end grain. If you want to extend the length of a piece of wood, a splice has to be made, or a support piece incorporated. The simplest splice is a stepped one, made by lapping one section of the wood over the other. Where this is not practical a piece of similar timber can often be let in, for instance at the back of a chair rail, where it is least visible. The solid piece of wood then supports the place where the break has occurred.

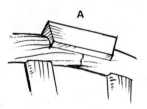

Spliced joint in chair rail. A new section of wood (A) has been glued in to bridge the break. When hard it can be planed to final shape

Number Four
Once a glue joint is made, it must be held rigid without any further movement until the glue is thoroughly hardened. As a rule of thumb this should be for at least twenty-four hours, although some glues do harden off in shorter periods, depending on the temperature and humidity.

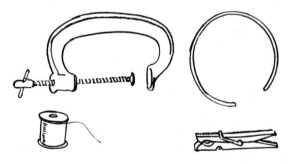

G. Cramp—cotton—Spring clothes pegs—and section of old upholstery spring

In order to support and hold rigid new joints a variety of clamps should be used. G cramps and sash cramps are the conventional method, but many alternatives can be improvised with a little ingenuity, using such things as Cellotape, spring clothes pegs, rope and string.

Now let us examine the adhesives that are available and in common use.

Firstly, Scotch Glue. This is bought in the form of sheet, pearl or powder. Pearl is most likely the most convenient to use. First the glue particles (or pearls) must be covered with water and soaked for eight to twelve hours. This is best done in a proper glue pot which is the equivalent of a double saucepan, or failing that, a suitable clean tin or jam jar. Animal glue should never be allowed to boil, so, after soaking, it is heated in a water jacketed container. The jam jar or tin in a saucepan over a gas ring will suffice, the bottom of the tin being separated from the bottom of the saucepan with a metal fret or a piece of wood.

When heated the glue should be the consistency of pouring cream. You can add more water to it to get the viscosity right. When the last drops of glue return to the glue brush rather than falling back into the pot you know it is ready for use.

When glueing large surfaces, or on a cold day, the surfaces to be glued should be warmed, otherwise the glue will start to set too soon. Cramps should immediately be applied and tightened to squeeze the excess glue from the joint. The less glue used the better. Excess glue can be wiped off with a damp rag.

Resin Adhesives

These glues set extremely securely and are either waterproof or highly water resistant. The only disadvantage they suffer is that they have a limited 'pot life', hardened off within an hour or so of being mixed. In consequence you must only mix up as much as you are going to use for immediate needs and estimating quantities can be tricky.

Cascamite comes in the form of a dry, white powder which contains both glue and hardener and is only activated when water is added. Like all other resin glues, the higher the temperature, the quicker it sets and setting can be accelerated by the application of warmth.

Aerolite 306 is also a white powder which is used in conjunction with an acid hardening agent. If you mix the powder with water and only apply the liquid hardener to one surface of the wood just before jointing, the powder–water mixture can be kept for a few days satisfactorily.

Polyvinyl Acetate Glues. These are extremely convenient to use as most are packed in a flexible plastic container and can be squirted out on to the surfaces to be glued. They are water soluble and have a slight disadvantage that they tend to 'creep' when under stress in one direction only. Nevertheless they are ideal for general use in the workshop.

Easiest available and thoroughly recommend are Evostick Resin W and Borden. Both are thick white liquids which need no mixing before application and have a very long life in their original containers.

Impact Adhesives

These are rubbery, jelly-like substances used when sticking large areas, such as big sheets of veneers or plastic laminates to working surfaces.

Each surface is given a thin layer with a serrated scraper and allowed to stand until touch dry. Great care has to be taken with some brands as once the two surfaces are allowed to touch, they cannot be moved, even a little bit. Some recent developments of this type of adhesive do allow a short period of 'slip' for positioning. Particularly recommended is Thixofix, made by Dunlop.

Epoxy Resin Adhesives

These usually come in two tubes, equal parts being mixed before application. They are not generally suitable for use in woodwork, but are very effective when securing brass inlays or stringing. Araldite is the most universally available.

Chapter 4

VENEER REPAIRS

Perhaps the most common of all damage to furniture are those of veneers, as a very considerable proportion of all furniture of the 18th and 19th Century were of veneer construction.

Eighteenth Century furniture was made with very thick, hand-sawn veneers, some of it one-eighth of an inch thick, or sometimes even more. Early Victorian furniture was made with machine-sawn veneers, slightly thinner and more uniform in thickness, and in late Victorian and Edwardian furniture very thin knife-cut veneers were frequently employed. This, incidentally, is one of your clues for dating furniture.

The repair of veneer damage varies from very simple to extremely complex. Fortunately the bulk of veneer troubles are relatively easy to put right.

The most common damage is broken corners and chipped edges, caused by knocks and repeated handling, obviously just in the places where the damage is most noticable. Whenever possible, secure the broken pieces temporarily with a strip of Cellotape until a permanent repair can be made. This will save you the trouble and time of finding and shaping a new piece to replace the broken area. This brings you face to face with the problem of where to find suitable veneers for repairs. Most professional restorers cut their own veneers on a hollow ground circular saw, or by hand, and this is the best way to obtain a good match of both grain and colour. We have already discussed the merits of building up a stock of old pieces of wood for repair purposes.

Failing this, many art and handicraft shops sell marquetry sets and small pieces of veneers of many woods designed for use in the making of marquetry pictures. This is an easy source of supply for small quantities.

When you want larger quantities, you must pay a visit to a veneer merchant. A short list is given in the restorers' directory at the end of the book, but the *Commercial Classified Trade Telephone Directory* for your area will tell you if there is a local Veneer merchant.

You may have to use thinner veneers for your repairs than those originally used. In this case two, or even three, layers may have to be laminated together. In all events, it is better for the veneer being used for repair to be slightly thicker than that used on the rest of the piece of furniture. After the glue has set, the new piece can be planed and sanded down to the exact height required.

When repairing broken corners and frayed edges, the first step is to cut away the ragged edges with a sharp, thin-bladed knife. A small Stanley knife is ideal for this purpose. Don't use a thick-bladed knife, as this tends to burr the edges of the cut, preventing you from making a clean and nearly invisible joint.

When cutting out to make clean edges for the repair, follow the pattern of the grain wherever possible. When you have to cut across the grain, make your cut an easy curve, rather than a straight line, as this will render the finished repair even less detectable. The eye picks up a straight line much more easily than a curve.

Next, carefully clean away all the old glue and wood chips that still may be adhering to the repair area. This can be done usually by scraping with a chisel of suitable size, or with a knife blade. Avoid wetting the area to loosen the glue if possible. If you do have to use water, use as little as possible, so as not to lift the veneer surrounding the repair area.

Next, make a paper pattern of the shape required for the repair. This is done in the same way as a child makes a facsimile of a coin, by placing a piece of paper over the area of repair and lightly pencilling over the surface, thus producing an outline of the missing veneer. The pattern is now cut out with a pair of scissors and fitted into the cavity to ensure a perfect fit.

Glue the pattern on to a suitable piece of veneer and cut out the shape with either a fine fretsaw, or better still, a sharp Stanley knife. When cutting out the piece with a knife, under-cut the jointing edges very slightly and leave a small surplus

C

A   B   D

Veneer repairs:
A. Cut out a suitably shaped area with smooth sides
B. The area with veneer removed and surfaces cleaned off
C. Using a paper pattern to fit hole, cut out new piece of veneer
D. Hold glued patch in position firmly with adhesive tape

on overhanging edges. Finally fit the new piece, adjusting it where necessary with a fine file or sandpaper held flat on a block of cork or wood.

When you are sure of the fit, glue it into place. The paper pattern can be left on until the joint has hardened, when it can be sanded off along with the surplus wood.

In most cases the best glue to use is Borden or Evostick

Resin W (or similar adhesive). For very small repairs you can use glue in tubes, such as UHU or Secotine.

Once the replacement piece has been finally positioned, the glue joint must not be broken. You can slide the piece around until the best possible fit is obtained. Once this has been done, the join must be subjected to pressure by cramping. The easiest way to do this in most cases, is to use Sellotape or masking tape. The most useful width of tape is $\frac{3}{4}''$ to $1''$. The technique is to place the end of the tape on part of the original surface and press it firmly home. Then stretch the tape slightly and bring the rest of the tape down across the repair area and where possible extend the tape to the area of original surface on the other side of the repair. On occasion you may have to carry the tape round the corner on to other surfaces of the piece of furniture. In this event, ensure that you do not pull the two glued surfaces apart. Now set the piece aside for at least twelve hours to allow the glue to harden thoroughly.

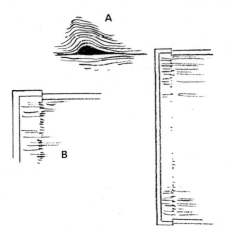

Bubbles in veneer, to be ironed down.
Stress marks in veneered table top due to shrinkage of carcase wood

Alternatively, a flat piece of scrap wood can be used in conjunction with a G cramp to exert pressure on the repair. In order to prevent the surplus glue that may be squeezed out from sticking to the pressure block, sandwich two or three layers of newspaper between it and the repair.

Where cross banding, or the veneer on drawer rails, has been damaged or chipped because of excessive wear caused by the drawer runners, cut out a complete section of the veneer and replace it, the new joint will be completely invisible if care is taken over the selection of the replacement wood.

In the case of worn drawer rails, the worn away groove in the carcase wood has to be repaired first. Alternatively, a second drawer runner can be fitted beside the existing one in many cases, thus preventing further wear in the groove which has already suffered many years of friction and wear.

Large Areas Over One Square Foot

Sometimes, in long neglected furniture, large areas of veneer are either so badly damaged that they cannot successfully be repaired or are completely lost. Here it is best to take out large sections, extending the full width of the original veneered surface and replace them with new, or matching old veneers taken from discarded furniture that is beyond repair.

The traditional method of laying veneers was with Scotch glue, using a veneering hammer. This is a task best tackled by a professional restorer, but you can undertake a task of this magnitude by using modern impact adhesives, such as Thixofix,

First, the old glue and dirt has to be cleaned from the surface of the carcase and rubbed down with glasspaper. Any small indentations or holes are then filled with a suitable stopper, such as Brummer.

When you are satisfied that the surface to be veneered is quite flat and free from dust, a piece of veneer of suitable size is prepared. Both the surface of the carcase and of the veneer are coated with the adhesive, using a serrated scraper. Your ironmonger will supply you with a plastic scraper free of charge when you buy a tin of adhesive. These scrapers leave just the right amount of glue on the surface. Lay them aside for about fifteen minutes, until both coatings are touch dry.

Now carefully position the veneer edge against the existing veneer on the carcase without letting the two coated surfaces come into contact. When you are sure that the position of the veneer is correct, lay the veneer quickly, making sure that no air bubbles are trapped beneath the veneer. You will be able to slide the veneer very slightly for a second or two with some modern impact adhesives, but once the two surfaces are in close contact, it is down for good. Firm pressure all over the surface of the new veneer with a soft rag or a roller will ensure complete adhesion and remove small pockets of trapped air.

Bubbles and Blisters
When veneered furniture is subjected to excessive damp, or sometimes alternatively to periods of excessive dry—for instance when a piece of furniture stands too near a radiator, or in a centrally heated house—veneers expand, break away from the securing glue, and blister. Glue joints also perish at the edges or joints and cause the veneer to lift slightly. By tapping the surfaces of a piece of furniture with your finger nails you can easily detect any areas where the veneers have broken free from the carcase wood.

In some cases the glue itself will have perished, which means that new glue will have to be used to cure the fault. It is, however, always worth while trying to iron back the offending areas. For small blisters, a warm soldering iron with a large flat surface may do the trick. A damp cloth on the surface of the wood between it and the iron introduces some moisture into the area and aids re-sticking. Finish off with the iron direct on to the wood. Where larger bubbles are encountered, an ordinary flat iron is the best tool to use. If you have an old electric iron, this is an ideal tool for 'ironing down'. Sometimes the bubble is badly distorted, or the veneer has swelled so much that it will not shrink back into the flat. When this occurs, you have to damp the surface with a hot, wet cloth for sufficient time to allow the moisture to penetrate. Softening the wood in this way prevents splintering and cracking, and may shrink it sufficiently for ironing down. Where this is not the case, a transverse cut must be made along the grain of the wood for the full length of the blister and one edge of the veneer must be allowed to override the other edge when ironing down. The excess overlap is then trimmed off, leaving an invisible seam.

This ironing down process destroys the polish on the surface of the veneer. It is now necessary to remove all the old polish and prepare the surface for repolishing, but in most cases, when veneers have bubbled, there is hardly any polish left on the piece of furniture, so no great amount of extra work is created by the process.

When you find that the veneer will not stick back into place again, this means that the old glue is so far perished that it cannot be revived. New glue therefore has to be introduced between the veneer and the carcase wood. A similar cut along the bubble is made as described above and glue is introduced into the cavity on palette knife, or a suitable slip of scrap veneer. The joint now has to be held in place with a pressure block, separated from the surface with newspaper to prevent the excess glue from glueing the block to the surface.

The most difficult to repair faults to veneers is when a carcase panel has shrunk or moved in the framework which prevents it from warping. This causes a tear in the veneer where the panel is grooved into the end framing. Here a decision has to be made on whether to leave the fault, regarding it as an honourable mark of age, or alternatively, to conceal it as best you may.

The best technique is to remove the polish and rub down the raised edges with fine garnet or sandpaper on a cork block. Clean out all the dust, fill the torn holes with Brummer stopper of a suitable colour, and then repolish. Certainly this treatment makes the damage less visible and reduces the chances of further damage. With luck the stress marks may become almost completely invisible, but the whole surface will have to be repolished to achieve this. In practice it is better to fill the holes with a slightly lighter filler and colour down with pigmented paints or stains as a better match can be achieved in this way.

On occasion sections of inlays, stringing and ornamental cross bandings are found to be missing. Although these can be purchased from such dealers as Crispin & Son of Curtain Road, London E.C.1, almost invariably an exact match cannot be obtained. Short of making up a length as replacement, it is best and quickest to inlay a piece of sycamore or similar light coloured wood of suitable grain and paint or draw the pattern in with water colour paints; felt tip, or suitably coloured ball point pens. When polished over it is amazing how invisible such repairs become.

Armed with the information contained in this chapter, you can tackle pretty nearly any kind of veneer repair. Do not be too concerned about the variation of colours caused by introducing new pieces of wood into old furniture, the problem of colouring is fully covered in the appropriate chapter further on in this book. One thing that you must always bear in mind is that you will not see the full results of your endeavours until you have completed the last process of the restoration.

It is very easy for the beginner to lose heart because progress is not immediately recognisable. Patience, as you all know, is a virtue easy to talk about, but very hard to practice. Attention to detail at every stage pays big dividends, so make sure you have completed every detail of veneer repairs before going on to the next stage. So many beginners think they have failed, when they have only failed to go on long enough with the finishing processes to achieve a perfect job.

Chapter 5

MOULDINGS AND BEADINGS

Mouldings and beadings are thin strips of wood that are applied to furniture, either to add decoration or to cover up joints in the wood of the carcase or the veneer covering. Mouldings are shaped or carved, sometimes quite intricately; beadings are plain strips of wood performing the same functions as mouldings.

By their very nature, mouldings and beadings lend themselves to damage as they are the most vulnerable to catching on clothing and dusters, or being splintered during removals. Remember that it is most important that current breakages should be carefully held back in place with adhesive tape until you can get round to making a permanent repair.

The one thing that you can be certain about in these days of standardisation is that you will not be able to buy from a timber merchant or do-it-yourself shop a length of moulding to match the pattern you require, so you are going to have to fashion it yourself, but do not despair, this is not a terribly difficult task. The way you go about it depends on how much is missing.

Fortunately, in most cases, only a few inches are required. The first thing you have to do is to prepare the broken area by making all the edges square and clean. If a section of moulding has been shattered or broken off, make a diagonal cut with a Gents' Back Saw or a tennon saw right through the moulding, taking care not to cut into the carcase and clean the area thoroughly with a chisel, making sure that all the old glue is removed and the surface where the new piece of moulding has to be fixed is absolutely flat. If the damage is on a corner, take a wedge-shaped cut out. If the damaged area is in the centre of a moulding, or a section of a radius (like a piece on a pie-crust table) make the aperture wedge-shaped, so that the new section can be slid into place until it makes a tight fit.

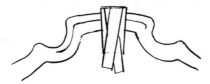

Break in pie crust table. The wedge-shaped piece is held in place with adhesive tape and formed to final shape when glue is hard

Do not make any attempt to shape the piece used for the repair before glueing it into place; just fashion it on the surfaces that are going to be glued to make a perfect fit, leaving a

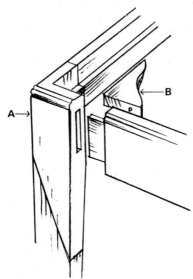

A. A new piece spliced in to replace shattered top of chair leg.
B. Strengthening block in angle of chair rail

generous overhang all round to be planed and rasped down after fixing. Of course, you must fabricate the new piece from similar wood as the original moulding, with similar grain, running in the right direction.

After the glue joint has hardened thoroughly, you can start to shape it. Start off with a hand plane and chisel, taking care not to remove too much of the surplus wood. Then work with rasps of suitable shape, a gouge where concave areas have to be removed, and finish off with fine files and finally sandpaper of increasingly fine texture. For difficult and intricate places you can wrap the sandpaper round a suitably shaped piece of softwood to achieve a perfect match of the sections.

For new lengths of matching moulding over a foot or so in length it is quicker to use a scratchstock. This is a tool that you will have to make yourself, but one can be made in an hour or so quite easily, and once you have it, it can be used time and time again. In the 17th and 18th Century all small mouldings were made with this tool and it is amazing how quick and efficient it is.

It looks rather like an old-fashioned spokeshave and you make it from a piece of hardwood (mahogany or beech are suitable) starting with a piece about $3'' \times \frac{3}{4}''$ about 15 inches long.

Draw out a pattern from the illustration and cut out the shape with a coping saw (or bandsaw if you have one). Now make the two handles at either end comfortable to hold by rounding over the edges. Next make the retaining block from $\frac{1}{2}'' \times 1\frac{1}{4}''$ wood about $3\frac{1}{2}''$ long. Position this block and hold it with a cramp while you drill a $\frac{3}{4}''$ diameter hole through the tool and the block. These holes accommodate two small carriage bolts and are retained with wing nuts.

The irons are made from pieces of old saw blades, steel rules or any old pieces of tempered steel. They take only a few minutes to grind to shape on a carborundum stone. Finally, true up with a set of fine cut warding or key files. The profile required is marked out with a scribe or bradawl and when the shape has been roughly filed out, the finishing is done by matching up to a section of the existing moulding.

The iron is then secured in the wooden tool, close up to the shoulder as shewn in the illustration and is drawn along a length of square or suitable sectioned wood, held in a vice or by a bench stop. A six or eight foot length of moulding can be shaped in less than half-an-hour. The blade does not need sharpening at all—but it must be cleared frequently of shavings and sawdust. In order to prevent the wood from tearing or furring up, the tool should be drawn in the direction of the grain. During the finalstages only light pressure is needed to bring up quite a respectable polish finish. The harder the wood, the easier it is to shape the moulding, providing it is free from knots and cross grain. The same tool can be used to put a reeded finish on the edge of tables, chests of drawers, etc.

Cocked Beads
Most 18th Century drawers were made with a rounded bead standing proud of all the front edges. These beadings are secured in a channel cut into the sides and bottom of the drawers, and across the full depth of the top edge. Because

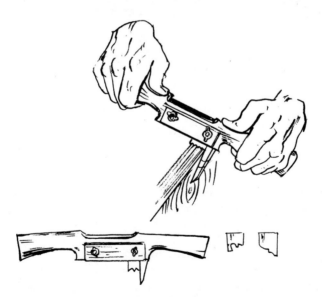

Scratch stock with cutters made from old saw blades

49

they stick out from the flat surface of the drawer front, they are very liable to damage and so are worthy of special mention.

Cocked beadings of various sizes are available from some specialised timber merchants supplying the furniture trade, but are also very easy to make. Most timber yards will run off a few metres of rectangular wood of suitable dimensions if you do not have a small bandsaw or do-it-yourself circular saw. All you have to do is round the forward edge with sandpaper.

When repairing broken cocked beads, cut off the broken end with a fine tooth saw and fit a new section, mitreing the joints at the drawer corners. The new section is secured with glue and veneer pins and smoothed down with sandpaper to make a fit to the existing bead.

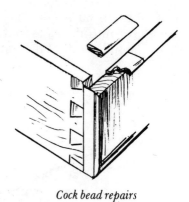

Cock bead repairs

Cross Banding and Cross Grain Mouldings

All cross banding, and some mouldings, principally from the walnut period (1660–1720) are worked on end grain. This gives a very interesting configuration in the wood, but over a period they are liable to shrinkage and, because they are invariably worked from short lengths of timber, the joints tend to open up. Occasionally, when they are recessed in a rebate, veneer is also laid over the edge of the moulding, causing the edge of the veneer to chip when the moulding is broken.

Fortunately repairs in cross-grained mouldings do not show at all if care is taken over the repair, due to the variation in colour of the end grain.

Where there are only slight cracks in a moulding of this type, slips of veneer can be glued into the cracks and, when dry, taken down to the correct profile. If necessary, the crack can be opened and cleaned by making a cut with a Gents' back, or fine tooth tenon saw. If whole sections are missing, suitable pieces of similar wood have to be cut and glued into the recess. When dry they can be cut down to shape with a sharp hand plane and finally sandpapered flush. Broken edges of veneers can sometimes be trimmed back slightly with a sharp knife and a steel straight edge, but if the chips are too pronounced, a veneer repair must be done as well, after the moulding repair has been completed.

Chapter 6

SPLITS BREAKS AND HOLES

Some furniture, particularly that built from solid unveneered wood, when it gets old, develops splits. Depending on the size, these are corrected by slightly different treatments. Very slight splits can often be pulled together with a sash cramp after glue has been spread inside the split.

Big splits, however, have to be treated somewhat differently as they are likely to spring open again, often breaking in a different place from the glued joint. A medium size split, particularly when the wood has warped slightly so that the two edges do not go back together easily, can be held in position by cutting a recess in the under-side about two to three inches long and a quarter of an inch deep, and glueing a piece of wood with the grain running in the opposite direction into the recess. The split is held in correct position with a cramp. To ensure that the two sides of the split come accurately together, two pieces of flat board can be cramped, one on either side of the split (separated from the surface by a sheet of newspaper to ensure that they do not stick).

In the case of large cracks, the best course is to insert a sliver of wood suitably tapered to the shape of the split and glue and cramp it in place. After the glue has dried the excess wood can be planed off and sandpapered down until it is quite level.

In cases where the planks making up a table top or the top of a chest have separated, or partially separated, due to the failure of the original glue joint, it is usually necessary to take the whole table top to pieces in order to clean out the dust, fluff, grease and other dirt that has accumulated. With modern adhesives it is not usually necessary to dowel these joints into place and, in any case, the accurate positioning of dowels is a difficult operation unless you possess a dowelling jig. It may be necessary to take a very fine shaving from each of the edges that have to be joined but, if you do this, a long shooting plane is recommended, otherwise it is difficult to achieve an exact fit of the two planks. Again, the device of cramping spare wood on either side of the joint is used to ensure exact positioning and sash cramps are required to put pressure on the joint.

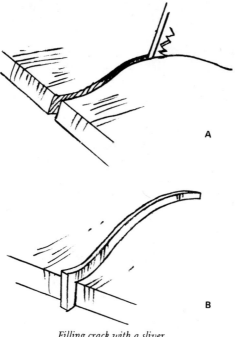

Filling crack with a sliver.
A. Crack opened at thin end with saw.
B. Sliver inserted.

It is always important to wipe away as much as possible of the surplus glue squeezed out from a joint with a damp cloth but, obviously, this is impossible underneath the supporting battens which again are prevented from sticking to the surface by the use of newspaper.

In some furniture a panel construction is used; this is particularly to be found in early oak furniture. These panels were originally made as a loose fit in the frames, thus allowing for expansion and contraction to take place. Where splits occur in these panels it is usually best to repair them by glueing a strip of new wood into the gap, but where the panels are broken into two halves and cannot easily be removed from its frame, the two broken edges can be coated with glue by working it into the crack with a palette knife or a piece of veneer. Then the two halves can be forced together with a sharp tool such as an awl, being dug into the inside or back of the panel, and while the two haves are being held together a panel pin is driven temporarily into the panel close to the edge of the frame, thus acting as a wedging device, to be removed as soon as the glue has hardened.

Small splits and screw holes in unobtrusive places can always be filled with Brummer stopper of an appropriate colouring and then shaded in with wood stains, but occasionally you find large screw or nail holes on the tops of pieces of furniture where the use of stopper would be so obvious as to make it unacceptable. When faced with this problem it is far better to inlay an elliptical piece of wood into the surface.

First find a piece of suitable wood about half to three-quarter inches thick and shape it into a pointed oval with very slightly tapered sides. Use this piece of wood as a template to mark out the area to be cut away. Using a sharp knife cut as deeply into the wood as you can, keeping the outer edges sharp and right angled. Now cut away the wood surrounding the offending screw hole right up to the edge of your elliptical cut with a sharp chisel, finishing off the bottom of the resulting hole as flat as it is possible to make it. Run a small quantity of glue around the edges and over the bottom of this incision and then drive the wedge shaped lozenge into the hole with a mallet. You need not worry about bruising the wood as your cut will be at the most $\frac{1}{4}$ inch deep and there is a large surplus to be planed off when the glue has dried. Make sure, of course, that you have achieved a really tight fit on the edges by trying the piece before final glueing but do not drive it home, as it will be difficult to remove again. Providing you have selected a suitable piece of wood for this type of repair, you will find that it is, when finished, almost completely invisible.

Chapter 7

BROKEN LEGS AND ARMS

Wherever possible it is, of course, best to preserve and refix broken legs and arms. With new breaks, a simple glue joint with a strong adhesive, such as Cascamite, will make a virtually invisible repair. It is surprising how most people, without experience, distrust the ability of good modern glues to make an effective joint, but this has already been discussed in an earlier chapter. Providing, however, that there is plenty of clean surface to come into close contact, glueing the two halves together is often effective and, after the joint is thoroughly hardened any rough edges or unevenness can be sandpapered down, small gaps can be filled with Brummer stopper. When repolished the joint will be invisible, except to very close examination.

It is essential, of course, for the new joint to be suitably clamped while drying, and considerable ingenuity is often called for. A later chapter is devoted to these techniques.

Quite frequently leg and arm repairs require the fashioning and splicing in of a new piece of wood. The important thing is to make a good strong joint first. The planing and sanding down to correct size and shape can be left until later.

The making of a strong joint calls for the employment of a little simple mechanics and geometry. First study the way the grain runs. In sabre-legged chairs, for instance, on one side the grain is long and has strength, on the other the grain is short and liable to snap under stress.

If you design your new joint in the form of a Z with hooked ends, you will achieve the greatest strength. Remember that you cannot make a good glue joint on end grain, so the longest part of the join should be with the grain of both pieces of timber lying parallel.

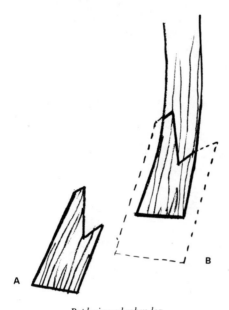

Replacing a broken leg.
A. First cut new join
B. Glue in place. When dry shape to match other leg

First you must cut out roughly a new section of leg (A) and mark and cut out the area of the join. Using this piece of wood as a template, the cuts in the broken leg can be marked out and then cut out to make an exact join. (B) The two pieces are now glued and cramped in place, and then the surplus timber is trimmed off to the correct shape of the leg. In order to do this, make a paper pattern from the other leg.

Broken, turned table legs are best dowelled together with as large a wooden dowel or peg as it will accommodate. If it is a jagged break, first glue the two parts together and, when dry, saw the leg off again at a place near to the temporary repair where it will not show, as at a groove in the turning. The place for the dowel hole now has to be determined in the centre of the leg. This can be done in two ways.

(A). A pin is driven in to one section of the leg, nearly home, with about 3/16th″ protruding and the pin head sharpened with a file. The leg is now pushed on to the stump. The sharpened pin makes a small hole which gives you centre for the drilling operation. Draw out the pin from the leg and again you have an accurately positioned centre for drilling the dowel hole.

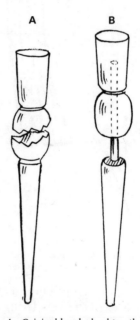

A. *Original break glued together.*
B. *Clean cut made elsewhere and dowel inserted past original break to give strength and support*

The dowel itself has to be cut about $\frac{1}{4}″$ shorter than the sum of the depths of the two dowel holes. Both ends are rounded off with a rasp and it is then held in a vice while a saw cut is made the full length of the prepared dowel. This shallow saw cut is the escape channel through which the surplus glue will be extruded when the two parts are forced together. Glue is applied to both dowel holes and the surfaces which are to come in contact with each other. The dowel has to be long enough to extend well beyond the position of the previous break.

The second method of finding centre is to use a compass, fixed at roughly the diameter of the leg and marked from several positions on the circumference to determine exact centre on both parts of the leg.

With some legs, particularly cabriole and carved tripod legs, the break may be at such an oblique angle that the repair can be affected by driving two or more dowels through a normal glue joint. This gives additional strength to an area where there is natural weakness, due to the way the grain in the wood runs. The alternative is to chisel a channel from the back, or some other unobtrusive part of the leg, and glue in a suitably shaped loose tenon.

Dowels used to repair oblique break

The use of loose tenons is a very useful device for making very strong repairs in cases where awkward joints are called for. It is therefore important to understand the mechanics of a mortice and tenon joint, one of the commonest methods of jointing wood used in cabinet making.

To make a mortice and tenon joint, a mortice gauge is used

to ensure accuracy in marking out. The two points of the gauge are set to span exactly the width of the chisel to be used

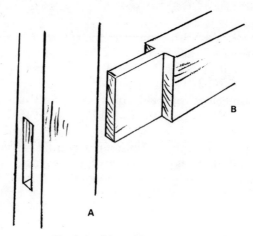

Mortice and tenon joint

for cutting the mortice (A). Once set, the gauge is used to mark out both the mortice and the tenon (B). The mortice slot is now chopped out with a mortice chisel and the tenon cut with a tenon saw, making certain that the saw cuts on the outside of the scribe lines to ensure a tight fit. When glued and fitted together a mortice and tenon joint is the strongest of T joints that can be made. It is employed in many ways, such as fixing of chair rails, chair splats, in fact anywhere that a right-angled join is required.

Loose tenon

The loose tenon employs exactly the same technique,

except that the tenon itself, instead of being cut into the end of one of the pieces of wood, is entirely separate and is inserted into a mortice channel cut to bridge both of the pieces of wood to be joined.

On some occasions this can be a through slot, cut with a saw. In some cases the channel has to be excavated with a suitable chisel without penetrating the front side of the work, thus concealing the repair as much as possible. In all cases fit the two parts together accurately and use a twin pointed mortice gauge to mark out accurately the location of the mortice channels.

A variation of this technique can be used when a break in a chair rail is to be mended. A section at the back of the rail can be sawn and chiselled away, leaving the front portion intact, except for the break. A piece of new wood can then be glued into the cavity, bridging the break and, when dry, shaped down to match the original contour of the rail.

Loose tenons can also be used to repair such troubles as chair seat rails where the joints have become smashed beyond repair. The seat corners can also be further strengthened by fixing corner brackets. These are made from hardwood, cut on the cross grain and shaped so that they can be screwed, as well as glued on to the seat rails to give maximum strength at a point of maximum stress. (See illustration p. 47)

The arms on elbow chairs can often pose a difficult problem. Uprights are usually screwed and glued to the seat rail. If the screw is inserted from the inside, it is invisible. If from the outside, it must be countersunk deep enough for the hole to be covered with a matching plug. The joint to the back of the chair is sometimes similarly secured with a screw, but on 18th Century chairs the joint is more often a mortice or a half lap T joint. When these have broken away, it is usually better to cut out the area of broken wood and insert a new piece. This can then be worked to form a well fitted new joint. The extra trouble taken is well rewarded, as makeshift joints do not usually last for long, and Brummer stopper or Plastic wood do not have sufficient strength to withstand constant wear and tear.

Tripod legs are another subject very prone to breakage due to constant leverage on the dovetailed slot in the upright pillar in which they are housed. It is quite a common occurrence for the wood forming the dovetail to break out, shattering the base of the pillar.

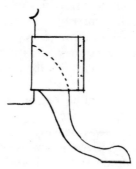

Cramping up box in position

The first problem is to release the leg. If part of the glue joint is still holding, the old glue has to be released. This can be achieved by perishing the glue artificially by irrigating the joint with methylated spirit. This has an instant effect, and the old glue can be heard cracking if the part is held near to your ear. Of course penetration of the meths to all parts of the joint has to be achieved, and it is sometimes necessary to drill fine holes into the joints. An oil can with a fine nozzle or, alternatively, an old plastic 'squeezy' bottle filled with meths is useful for this operation.

The leg can now be struck off with a mallet, protecting the leg from bruising with a piece of scrap timber. If it does not start to move at once, look for old nails and screws which have been used at some time to make rough and ready repairs. Alternatively, wooden dowels may have been employed, in which case they must be drilled out.

The joint must now be thoroughly cleaned of old glue and, if possible, the shattered shoulders of the dovetail glued back into place. Should this be impossible, new shoulders must be glued in and cut to shape. The legs may now be glued back into place one at a time, allowing each leg to harden thoroughly before fitting the next. If the fit is sloppy, the joint can be tightened up by inserting slivers of veneer between the shoulder and the dovetail on the leg, ensuring that the curved face of the leg fits snugly on to the central pillar. The cramping in position during the time that the glue is hardening presents a minor problem, and it is always best to make a shoe to fit the knee of the leg.

Take a piece of scrap wood, the same width as the leg, and mark and cut it out to an exact fit. Now tack a piece of hardboard or ply to each side of the block to fit over the sides of

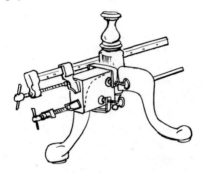

Holding tripod leg in position while reglueing

the leg. The whole shoe can now be held on the leg with G cramps. The block, thus secured, presents a square face for the location of the jaws of two sash cramps to secure the leg tightly to the central column. The same procedure is repeated for the two remaining legs.

Chapter 8

WEAR AND TEAR

Like everything else, furniture suffers over the years from fair wear and tear. Even furniture that has been very carefully looked after is subject to wear in moving parts, particularly drawer runners and dividers; table hinges and rule joints; slides of chests of drawers; and knuckle joints of gate leg tables. Chairs are particularly prone to wear and tear, specially if subjected to the strain of large children (and sometimes grown-ups) rocking on the back legs. It is with the repair of these defects that this chapter deals.

If you examine the bottom of a drawer, in all but those of the earliest oak period, you will find that they run on two strips of wood which are extensions of the two sides. Depending on how great the weight of your possessions kept in the drawers, and the frequency of their opening and closing, the drawer runners wear down over the years, and, at the same time, cut channels in the framework of the carcase.

The rate of this wear can be reduced considerably if the drawer runners are lubricated regularly (about once a year), by rubbing them with a candle. The coating of hard wax reduces the friction, and makes the drawers run in and out much more easily. This is a task which should be remembered and, in spite of being rather a nuisance, should be undertaken if you want to preserve your furniture as long as possible between renovations.

When drawer runners do wear down, the maximum friction, and greatest degree of wear, is always at the back of the drawers and the runners eventually become wedge-shaped, causing the drawers to tilt back slightly. This makes the front of a bureau or chest of drawers look badly made and the drawers ill-fitting. Once you are aware of this fault you will be surprised how conscious you become of the fact when looking at old furniture. Once corrected, the whole piece of furniture looks very much smarter.

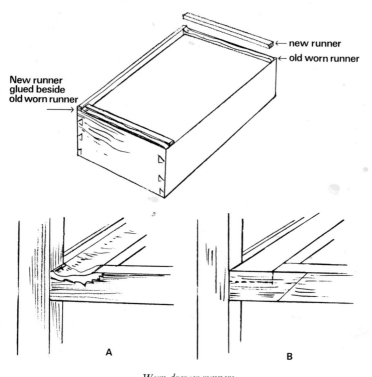

Worn drawer runners.
A. Worn drawer rail and broken veneer.
B. Rail replaced and veneer repaired

In many cases a very easy solution can be applied to correct this fault. In many cases the drawer supports in the carcase of the piece of furniture are wide enough for a new runner to be glued on to the bottom of the drawer, up against the old worn runner. The new runner thus does not run in the worn groove of the drawer rail and in consequence the drawer no longer tilts back at the top.

Sometimes, however, the rail is not wide enough to accommodate a second runner. In this case the existing runners will have to be made good. Firstly the worn portion of the runner has to be cut away and squared off. This can only be done with a chisel and bull-nosed plane, as care must be taken not to damage the front of the drawer. A new strip of hardwood can now be glued into place. It is always best to use hardwood, such as oak or beech, for replacement runners as they obviously will last longer and it is most important not to secure them with nails or screws because as further wear and tear takes place over the years, the steel heads will start to protrude and tear into the drawer rails on which they run.

In extreme cases the runners may have worn down so much that the bottom of the drawer has also been damaged. The drawer bottom is normally housed in parallel rebates cut in the drawer sides, and kept in place by one or two brads securing the back board to the back of the drawer. If these pins are pulled out, the whole drawer bottom will slide out as it is not glued into place. The repairs to the runners can then be completed and a new rebate cut into the drawer side to accommodate the bottom, which can be slid back into place.

If the drawer bottom has shrunk, an extra piece of wood of similar thickness can be put in. If it has warped, it is sometimes a good idea to glue a strip of linen or canvas over the gap to hold the edges together.

The problem of troughs or grooves in the drawer rails is a little more difficult to handle, as access for tools and your hands is often restricted. On drawer rails, the maximum wear is at the front of the drawer and may not extend very far back into the carcase. Where this is the case a rectangular channel has to be chiselled and sawn out to accommodate a new piece of hardwood fashioned to fill the worn trough. As the front of the drawer rails is likely to be veneered, the chances are that this veneer has been badly chipped, so the new section will have to be fitted far enough back to allow a new section of the veneer face to be spliced in after the major repair has been completed.

66

In very bad cases of wear, it is often quicker and easier to remove the whole rail, if the piece of furniture has a frame construction. The drawer rails are normally only glued in, so the whole side rail can be removed and replaced with a new one.

We have already dealt with cocked beads in the chapter on beadings and mouldings, but we still have to consider drawer stops. A drawer is prevented from sliding too far into the carcase by either a drawer stop, which is a small block of wood glued and pinned to the drawer rail, or by lipped drawer front where, instead of a cocked bead, a moulding is worked on the front edges of the drawer, overlapping the carcase and stopping the drawer from sliding too far into the carcase.

Drawer stops often get knocked off, or so badly worn that the drawer edge overrides them. The positioning of new stops is critical and the tool to use for this is a mortice gauge. The thickness of the front of the drawer can easily be measured off on the gauge and a mark made with it on the front drawer rail, giving an accurate position for the new stop which can be both glued and pinned into position.

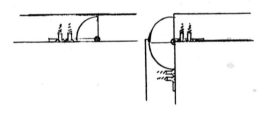

Rule joint. Note correct positioning of hinge

Rule joints on drop leaf tables were a refinement which became popular among 18th Century cabinet makers to hide the ugly gap visible when a simple square-edged leaf is let down. It is made up of a quarter round moulding worked on the edge of a table top which fits exactly a similar concave moulding on the underside of the drop leaf.

By this device, not only is there no gap between top and leaf when the latter is lowered: when the leaf is horizontal the majority of its weight is carried by the mouldings. Previously the weight was borne by the hinges and, in consequence, the screws tended to be pulled out over a period.

Swelling or distortion of the wood can cause rule joints to bind and this in turn causes the polish on the moulding to become scored, scratched and, in consequence, unsightly. Even worse, the very thin wood covering the knuckle of the hinge sometimes splinters, revealing the hinge peeping through a jagged hole. The reason for this is that the hinge has to be fitted with the knuckle uppermost and part of the wood of the quarter round bead has to be pared away to accommodate the knuckle.

Simple binding can easily be cured by removing the leaf and rubbing down with garnet paper or glass paper on a wooden rubber, shaped to fit the diameter of the moulding. Where the joint has been broken away, however, a new piece of matching wood must be spliced in, and to make a durable repair the break must be cut back a half-inch beyond either side of the hinge recess. A wedge shape cut allows you to make a tight fit with the replacement section. After the glue has dried, the surplus wood can be planed off and smoothed down and a suitable recess to accommodate the knuckle of the hinge is then worked with a small half-round gouge. It is important to leave sufficient space for the knuckle to rotate, and to cut a recess of exactly the right depth for the leaf of the hinge when the leaf is up.

The exact positioning of the hinge is important. This is easy to find if you are replacing the same hinge, but if new ones are to be fitted, care must be taken to ensure that centre of the knuckle is exactly below the shoulder of the quarter round moulding.

With all old hinge joints, you often find that the holes have become so enlarged that the screws do not hold firmly into the wood. Sometimes you can get away with plugging these holes with sharpened small dowels, glued into the old screw holes, but in bad cases it is better to reposition the hinges where the wood is sound and fill the old recesses by glueing in a suitable piece of wood.

Another way of overcoming the problem of enlarged screw holes is to use a larger (not longer) size screw. When this is done however, the countersunk recesses in the hinge should be enlarged with a metal cutting countersink bit, otherwise the heads of the screws will stand proud. This is not so important with table leaves, but on flush doors, coffer lids, cupboard doors, and the like, this will cause the hinges to spring, prevent the door from closing properly and, if forced shut, shatter or split the wood holding the screws.

When fitting new hinges it is essential to position them correctly, with the knuckle end protruding slightly. The recesses which accommodate the hinges must also be cut to the exact depth, so that the hinge is flush with the surrounding woodwork when the door or lid is open. If the recess is too deep, the door will not shut properly, if too shallow, a tight joint will not be made when the door is shut.

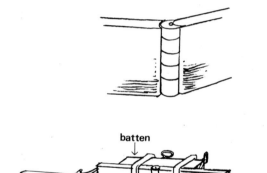

Broken knuckle joint. Note method of holding for removing worn pin, drilling out for fitting new larger pin

Knuckle joints are used instead of hinges on many card and tea tables where one or more leg swings out to support the open leaf. The main problem with these is the metal securing pin wearing away the supporting wood and the wood between each knuckle becoming worn away by friction. These joints have to be tight, as they rely on friction and tightness for their rigidity. The joint can be tightened up by knocking out the old metal pin, drilling out the worn hole about 1/16th" or 1/8th" larger and inserting a larger size pin to replace the old one. Remember that you must make a tight push-home fit. Where the knuckles are badly worn, the movement can be taken up by inserting washers between the knuckles or glueing slips of veneer on the worn faces. When drilling out the centre pin hole, both knuckles must be made rigid in their correct position by clamping a splint across the joint and securing with G cramps on both arms.

In extreme cases, knuckle joints are smashed beyond repair. If the task of making a new knuckle joint is too much for you to tackle, a repair can be made by replacing the knuckle with a suitable strap hinge. This, however, is not the kind of repair that will satisfy a dedicated restorer.

Chapter 9

ALTERATIONS

Earlier on we considered briefly the possibility of conversions and alterations of pieces of furniture which were either no longer in fashion or were no longer acceptable in your home because they were considered ugly. There are also dozens of examples of pieces of furniture which, with a little imagination, can be vastly improved by, quite often, very simple and minor alterations.

Perhaps the classic example of a very simple alteration altering the whole appearance of a piece of furniture is the changing of turned wooden handles for brass ones. It is interesting to note that originally most 17th and 18th Century furnitui e was fitted with cast or pressed brass handles, but our Victorian forebears, for some reason or other, disliked them and had them removed from their chests of drawers and desks, replacing them with turned wooden monstrosities. Nearly all the furniture built for the next sixty or seventy years also had turned wooden handles fitted. Very often, if you examine a piece of 18th Century furniture, you can see on the drawers the evidence of these changes in fashion in handles.

At all events, brass handles are now in favour, but here a word of caution does not come amiss—before you rip off the wooden handles on a piece of furniture, take a long look at it. In some cases the original handles are beautiful and well proportioned. This applies particularly to davenports and some small cabinets and the interiors of bureaux and secretaires. If these are fitted out with turned ivory handles especially, under no circumstances change them for brass knobs—even if you have to find a turner to copy the missing ones at what appears to be a high price.

Large, inelegant wooden handles are sometimes just threaded into the drawer front or retained with a wooden screw that goes through a smooth hole in the drawer, screwing into the knob itself and retained at the back of the drawer with a flanged head. If no glue has been used to secure them, handles can often be unscrewed with the additional persuasion of a pipe wrench or similar grip. Care has to be taken with tight knobs on veneered surfaces, or the veneer may be torn.

When the knobs are glued in, the first step is to chip away the shoulder with a chisel. This is easy as the grain in knobs always runs front to back. The remaining central dowel can then be cut off proud of the front with a chisel and then sanded down or, alternatively, can be twisted out of its hole. The hole in the drawer front has then to be plugged, unless a new handle with a back plate large enough to cover the hole is going to be used.

Reproduction brass handles in a large variety of styles are available but, alas, not from very many local ironmongery shops these days. There are, however, a number of specialist suppliers who will supply you by post and publish catalogues. It is best, however, if you can do so to go to their shops and make an on-the-spot selection of the handles best suited to your requirements.

Most handles consist of a back plate, a handle retained by a pair of threaded bosses, held in place by nuts. When fitting new handles to a chest or bureau, it is essential to measure the position of each fairly accurately. Nothing looks worse than a piece of furniture with its handles all slightly out of alignment. Such details make the difference between an amateurish and a professional job! The best way is to use a template made from some scrap wood or cardboard to position each backplate in turn from each side of the drawers. As most sets of drawers are graduated, the deepest at the bottom and the shallowest at the top, the centre position has to be found on each drawer and for this a mortice gauge, which can be quickly adjusted for each drawer, is the best tool.

Once the backplate is accurately positioned, the holes for the retaining screws and bosses can be marked with a bradawl and suitable holes drilled with a brace and bit. Once the handle has been secured with the retaining nuts, it is best to cut off the surplus threads with a hacksaw blade or a junior hacksaw. Better still, the nut can be hidden in a countersunk recess.

Construction of bracket foot. Note screw holes for fixing

Another peculiarity of Victorian taste was a love of turned feet. Much of the William and Mary and Queen Anne furniture was made with large, bulbous and usually beautiful turned feet, but most 18th Century bureaux, chests-of-drawers and cabinets were fitted with bracket feet. These feet either were stepped out about $\frac{1}{2}$-inch from the line of the carcase, or in some cases were in line with the sides and front. Sometimes the latter feet were made 'to splay out' in a graceful curve, adding to the charm of the piece of furniture.

Our Victorian ancestors quite frequently substituted rather ugly, thin-turned legs for the original bracket feet, often because the originals were badly damaged, more often to conform with current tastes. They also built large numbers of chests on the then fashionable legs. Today bracket feet are much more acceptable and the substitution of bracket feet for these legs, now rather ugly to contemporary eyes, is a worthwhile and fairly simple task.

First the old legs have to be removed—usually it is simplest merely to saw them off flush with the carcase. Next a piece of applied moulding has to be glued and pinned to the bottom of the carcase on the front and two sides. This can be an ordinary commercial moulding of any suitable design of about $\frac{1}{2}''$ section. While this is laid aside to allow the glue to harden a start can be made on the feet.

Presuming you are altering a mahogany chest, six identical feet have to be cut out from a $1''$ or $1\frac{1}{4}''$ plank. (Note from the drawing the direction of the grain.) To do this it is best to make a cardboard or plywood template as this speeds up the marking out and ensures conformity. These six legs are now cut out, on a bandsaw if you have one, otherwise with a coping saw. If you are using old wood, make sure that the legs are all cut with the previously polished face to the front. In other words, the separate feet have to be cut so that they are left and right handed. If you lay them out on the plank so that they fit one another, yoy will achieve this and save wood at the same time.

The corners of FOUR of them are now mitred so they fit snugly together.

Next you make four rectangular legs out of a piece of about $1\frac{1}{2}''$ softwood, making them about $\frac{1}{4}''$ longer than the feet. This is so that, when assembled, the legs are just that little bit longer, extending downwards so that they alone rest on the floor. This prevents subsequent breaking or chipping of the mahogany feet over the years.

The supporting leg and the two front feet are now assembled with glue and panel pins. (The pin holes can be later filled with Brummer stopper); and secured so that they bridge the new applied moulding and bottom of the carcase and are glued and screwed into position.

The two back feet are assembled in much the same way, except that the side of the foot (the mahogany one) is not mitred at the back edge and extends slightly beyond the pine leg far enough to make a flush joint with a simple pine foot which is attached to the back of the carcase. (There is no need to use mahogany for the back part of the back foot which does not show, and this is the way they were always made in the past).

The same procedure applies when making bracket feet for bow-fronted chests, except that the two front feet have to be constructed at something over 90°, to conform to the contour of the front of the chest. This requires a little bit more fitting to get the angles right, but can easily be achieved by trial and error.

Old dressing tables and wash hand stands are also suitable subjects for conversion into writing tables, sewing tables, etc. All that has to be done with these is to remove the superstructure of the mirror stand and occasional small drawers in the case of dressing tables, or the splash back on wash hand stands, and make good the top.

In an earlier chapter you have discovered how to insert losenge-shaped plugs to conceal screw holes. Some dressing table tops may have had their superstructure channelled into the top. Once it is removed, you are left with a trough running two thirds of the way around the, otherwise perfect, top.

One of several alternatives can be chosen to conceal this blemish. Sometimes the easiest way is to remove the top completely and reverse it, making the underside the top. This is only practical, of course, if the underside is unblemished and is only secured with either glue blocks or very few screws, when the holes can be satisfactorily plugged.

The solution which is most satisfying, however, is to extend the channel around the four sides of the top and to insert an inlay of contrasting wood. In order to extend the channel you will have to use a plough or combination plane with a blade of the same width as the original channel.

Although a combination plane is one of the most expensive of hand tools, it is one of the most useful if you are intending to take woodworking as a serious hobby. Although it looks a complicated tool, it is not really difficult to use, once you have become familiar with its use. It will, in addition to ploughing grooves, make rebates, cut mouldings, tongue and groove planks and perform a wide variety of operations quickly and efficiently.

The corners of the channel have to be finished off and cleaned out with a chisel, taking care to keep the angles sharp and accurately cut. Suitable strips of contrasting wood preferably of a lighter colour, can now be fitted and glued into the channel. Be sure to mitre the corners to make a professional job.

Even better than this, the table top can be cross banded. Cut the channel as before all round the table and then plane down all of the outside edge to slightly less than the depth of the veneer you intend to use for cross banding. This is normally about 1/16th", but can be deeper if you intend to use suitable hand cut veneers.

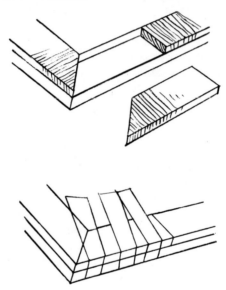

Cross banding repair. Adhesive tape used to secure patch while glue dries

Cross banding is made up of relatively narrow sections of veneers cut with the grain running front to back and laid side by side along the edges of a table or chest top. Care must be taken to get the proportions right, between $1\frac{1}{2}$" and $2\frac{1}{2}$" is normally most pleasing to the eye, but the width will, to some extent, be governed by the position of the original channel. The effect is much enhanced if a piece of boxwood or ebony stringing is inserted between the table top and the cross banding. This can be obtained from most veneer merchants.

The traditional method of laying cross banding is with Scotch glue, but on furniture of no great age or value, impact adhesives can be used quite effectively.

Any suitably contrasting wood can be used for cross banding. It is easiest to lay if there is wide colour variation in it, in consequence such exotic timbers as Kingwood, Satinwood, Yew, Harewood, Rosewood and Mulberry are first choices. Less ornamental, but equally pleasant effects can be obtained, however, by cross banding mahogany with the same wood, but with interesting figuring in the grain.

Following the cross banding and stringing operations, the surplus wood has to be removed with a fine set block plane and finally by sanding down. But here a word of warning. Never use a rotary disc sander on furniture. It will make circular score marks which are the very devil to remove. A reciprocating, or better still a belt sander can be used with safety, if you have one. Otherwise it is a case of elbow grease and, in all events, the final sanding should be done by hand. The piece of furniture is now ready for staining and polishing.

Possibly the most interesting pieces of furniture for conversion, and certainly the most versatile, are various designs of bedroom commodes, which were mentioned briefly in the preface. These are so many and varied that it is hardly practical to give detailed instructions for their conversion; in some cases considerable imagination, time and skill is required to turn them into useful items of household occasional furniture, but a few generalisations may be helpful.

When constructing drawers there is no need to use lapped dovetail joints, the traditional way of securing the sides to the fronts. A groove and rebate joint is quite satisfactory and takes a fraction of the time to make. (Here your combination plane will come in useful if you have one, if not a tenon saw and chisel will do the work nearly as quickly.)

Always construct drawers from fairly thin wood—best to use up the wood from old drawers whenever you can. If you use a drawer from a good piece of furniture as an example, you can refer to it when you get stuck on constructional detail.

Where you have a difficult piece to secure, like a new bottom for a workbox, do not overlook the use of glue blocks. These have been used traditionally for a couple of hundred years in carcase construction and overcome the necessity of using screws and panel pins—and of concealing the resulting holes. Never use screws or nails when an alternative fixing method can be employed, and small blocks of wood, coated with glue and rubbed firmly on to both surfaces to be joined make a very secure joint.

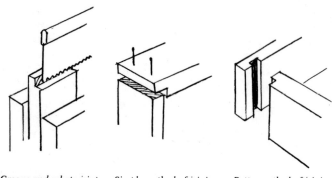

Groove and rebate joint.   *Simple method of joining*   *Better method of joining*
Cutting the rebate   *to side*   *to side*

Remember that it is essential to secure the piece of wood that you are working on properly. If you fail to do this the quality of your work will suffer. Besides a bench vice, buy or make yourself a bench stop, a bench hook, and invest in a bench holdfast. When you have a difficult or intricate piece of work on, make a jig if all else fails.

The above remarks will, I hope, be useful and may not be found in most books on joinery and cabinet making. The object of this book, remember, is not to teach you carpentry. If you feel that you need a book of reference to help you with details of woodwork practice, there are many excellent ones on the market. Stobart & Son Ltd. of 67–73 Worship Street, London EC2A 2EL, are specialist booksellers of publications on woodworking and handicrafts and will send you their specialist list on application.

Chapter 10

HOW TO HOLD IT STEADY

This chapter is divided into two parts, the first on how to use
the various types of cramps and securing devices to best advantage while glue joints are drying. The second part deals
with useful devices for holding work steady when fashioning
it to correct shape and size.

Both of these tasks are of vital importance and often call for
considerable ingenuity. Once, however, you have grasped the
principles and appreciated fully how much time and frustration you can save by the intelligent use of holding and
securing aids, you will stop wishing that you had been blessed
with a third hand.

Apart from the holding devices you can buy in a tool shop,
there are numerous ways in which you can improvise, but first
let us examine all of the available devices.

The most common are G cramps and thumb screws
which are used for holding relatively small parts together.
Thumb screws have a span of anything up to four inches and
G cramps can be obtained with an opening of between three
and eighteen inches.

Next come sash cramps and ratchet cramps or bar
cramps. The former can be obtained from two feet to six feet
in length and the latter with a span of up to two feet. These are
used for such tasks as holding table tops and carcases together
and for securing large frames.

A different kind of cramp is a webb cramp which consists of about 12 feet of nylon or cotton webbing with a metal

ratchet fastener which is tightened with a spanner or screw-driver. It is used for holding several elements in place at the same time, or on round or irregular work.

This is the sum of the commercially available holding devices which you will find in tool shops. It by no means exhausts the means you can employ for holding things in place temporarily.

Extremely useful for small articles are Cellotape and masking tape. These are both self-adhesive and can be used for all manner of small holding jobs. It is particularly useful for veneer and beading repairs.

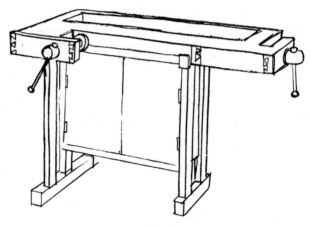

A modern bench

Old upholstery springs, when cut up into hoops, are extremely versatile in use as is twine, thread and clothes line, which can either be wound round joints or used as tour-niquets to hold parts together. Bulldog clips, spring clothes pegs, elastic bands, sections of old motor car tyre inner tubes, in fact, anything with a spring in it can all be brought into ser-vice as holding and clamping devices.

Most important, however, is to appreciate fully that any holding device must pull in the right direction. It is very easy to pull a joint out of square if pressure is exerted in even a slightly wrong direction. To overcome these problems the use of jigs or positioning blocks is called for. They can be made specially for specific jobs as they are required and only take a few minutes to fashion. Normally they are held in position with a handscrew or G cramp, allowing a sash cramp to be employed to exert a straight pull in the correct direction.

In this way round corners can be made square, purchase can be obtained on curved areas, and obtuse or acute angles can be made into right angles.

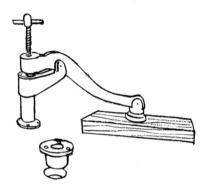

Bench holdfast

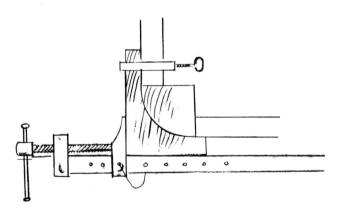

Squaring off a rounded corner

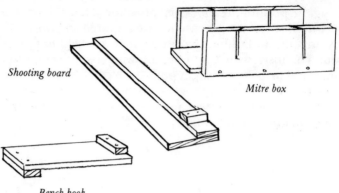

Shooting board

Mitre box

Bench hook

Equally as important is your ability to hold your work steady while you are shaping it. Your bench must therefore be equipped with a series of holding devices. A good carpenter's vice is possibly the first essential, but if you can provide yourself with a carpenter's bench fitted with an end screw, as well as a vice, you will find work much easier. The end screw can be used both as a second vice, and also to operate an adjustable Bench Stop. Fit an Eclipse bench holdfast and you have a third holding device.

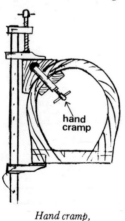

*Hand cramp,
holding a round chair back*

Wedges used to correct angles on a chair base

82

Other holding or steadying devices which you can either make for yourself or possibly buy are a bench hook for use when sawing timber at right angles with a tenon saw, a shooting board for planing and a mitre box for cutting at 45° and 90° angles.

Finally, it cannot be too strongly emphasised that, in order to avoid frustration and ensure safety when using edge tools, suitable holding devices must be incorporated in your workshop. Before attempting to glue or join parts together, you must equip yourself with an adequate number of cramps and other devices and when faced with a difficult cramping problem, use your ingenuity to devise suitable jigs to ensure even pressure all over the areas to be joined.

Chapter 11

BLEACHING, STAINING AND COLOURING

Once you are satisfied that all of the necessary repairs have been completed and that surfaces have been stripped of all old dirt, perished French polish or other finishes, the time has come to refinish the piece of furniture.

In spite of stripping and cleaning down, you may still find ink marks and other stains on some surfaces. In addition, there may remain in the wood old colouring agents which are unacceptable by today's standards. Our Victorian forebears were particularly prone to colouring up mahogany furniture with purple and deep red stains and, although stripping may have removed much of these offending dyes, a residue may be retained in the wood.

Today a light honey or hay colour is considered to be the most acceptable colouring for Mahogany furniture, a warm brown for Oak and a contrasting brown to honey for Walnut. Finishes should look as natural as possible, and any antique or near antique piece of furniture should have the warm sheen of persistent waxing and constant care.

As any housewife will know, you cannot stain or dye anything lighter than its original colour, so on occasion bleaching out of both stains and dark colours is called for, before recolouring to the desired tone.

A variety of bleaches are available, but as an all-purpose stand by, Oxalic acid is recommended. This can be obtained from most chemists in the form of white crystals which readily dissolve in hot water (one heaped tablespoon to a quart). This solution should be scrubbed into the surface of the wood with medium grade steel wool. If the surface has recently been stripped, some initial difficulty in securing penetration of the surface may be encountered, but a few seconds scrubbing with the steel wool will achieve thorough wetting. The whole surface should be treated, but special attention should, of course, be given to areas of staining. If only the stained areas are treated a light patch will result and you will have difficulty in restoring a uniform shade.

Do not be discouraged if, at first, the bleach appears to have little effect on some persistent stains. Scrub away at them, and if they appear to resist, allow the solution to dry on the surface for an hour. This will leave a horrible grey scum on the wood, which will quickly wash off with warm water. If the stains have not quite disappeared, a second application may be necessary.

After treatment with oxalic acid, great care must be taken to remove all trace of any residue by thorough washing with clean water and at least twenty four hours be allowed for thorough drying out.

As an alternative, peroxide of hydrogen (as used by hairdressers) or even household bleaches can be used, but the action of these materials is much more gentle and they are not nearly as effective as oxalic acid for the removal of ink stains.

When it is desirable to remove even more colour from furniture, you may have to resort to the use of specially formulated bleaches. One of the best is Gedges Original Ultrableach. This material has to be mixed with ·880 Ammonia just before application and, if two or three applications are made, will remove all colour from most timbers. Extreme care has to be exercised in thorough neutralisation, and some difficulty may be found in recolouring after a complete bleach-out.

Two types of stains are normally used for colouring furniture woods. One based on water solutions and one on spirit or naptha. By far the most satisfactory types are the water based stains, several of which have a chemical as well as a dyeing action. They have the great advantage, unlike the spirit stains, of being highly resistant to fading in sunlight. They also have the disadvantage of lifting the grain of the wood, necessitating rubbing down with fine garnet paper after staining. This disadvantage is not found with spirit stains. As a consequence, spirit stains are much more widely used these days as less time has to be expended on staining when they are used, and the application of a slightly darker tone compensates for the fading which must be expected.

Water stains should be used, however, where important pieces of furniture are being restored. These are the traditional stains and, as we know, the closer we adhere to original practices, the better, as far as antique furniture is concerned.

First you must appreciate that stains have different effects on different woods. They even have different effects on the same varieties of wood, so it is always advisable to carry out a test experiment; first on a similar piece of scrap wood, then on an unobtrusive area of the piece to be coloured.

Keep your stocks of stains in saturated solutions, by dissolving as much as you can in warm water and then allowing the surplus to crystallise out as the water cools. These saturated solutions can then be diluted to half, a quarter or even an eighth strength, as required, to give the desired tone. All water-based stains can be mixed together to give a desired colour, or can be used one on top of the other.

The traditional method of colouring was by the process known as 'fuming'. Originally mahogany furniture was coloured by placing it in an airtight room, known as a fuming chamber, and placing shallow bowls of strong ammonia over a candle or lamp flame in the room before sealing. The heat drove off the ammonia gas which has the action of developing out the natural red colouring in the wood and bringing it to the surface. The process also emphasises the variation of grain in the wood, bringing out the natural beauty of the figure in the wood.

Today, fuming in this way is no longer used. Instead we apply liquid ammonia to the surface of the wood with a soft, fluff-free cotton rag, and leave it for two or three hours before washing off with water.

Ammonia produces the red tones. Other commonly used 'fumes' are solutions of washing soda and Bichromate of Potash. Washing soda gives a pleasant grey effect and Bichromate of Potash is a strong orange-yellow agent. Tumeric, as used in mustard pickles and chutneys, is a strong yellow dye. Vandyke Crystals (mixed with boiling water) make a cold brown colour. All these colouring materials can be diluted with cold water to reduce this intensity. All the stains and fumes may be used in conjunction and Red Lead and Lamp Black, which are pigments, may also be added to enrich and darken the stains, but pigments must be used with restraint to avoid a 'painted' effect as pigments are opaque and, to some extent, are bound to obscure the natural beauty and grain of the wood.

Other pigment colours can also be used to complete the colouring, particularly when shading in is desirable. For instance, in moulding, carving and such places as drawer corners a gradation of colour is often desirable to bring out highlights. These effects are applied after basic staining has been completed. The most satisfactory method of application is to mix a little of the finely powdered pigments with either french polish, diluted 50/50 with methylated spirit or with Gedges liquid grain filling medium which is sold under the name of Duraxcote.

The pigments which you will find most useful are Red Lead and Lamp Black, already mentioned as additives to stains; Yellow Ochre, Lemon Chrome, Turkey and Brown Umbers, Prussian Blue and Ultramarine; Crimson Lake, Raw Sienna, Brunswick and Rose Pink (to give warm red and pink tones).

Spirit or Naptha Stains are the alternative to the traditional colouring materials. As mentioned before, they are prone to fading, but they are often used because they are quick and easy to apply. The best method is to blend your own shades of stain by making solutions of them in either solvent naptha or methylated spirits.

Spirit colours also come in fine powder form and are, in the main, aniline dyes. You need to have a range of these for blending the various shades and here is a list of those most useful for colouring wood:

Spirit Black
Spirit Yellow
Alcover Orange
Bismark Brown
Magenta
Chrysadine
Aniline Green

If they are kept in a fairly strong solution, ready mixed in methylated spirit, they can be thinned as required. A little French Polish or Gedges Duraxcote can be added to fix them temporarily when they are applied to the wood.

Tumeric, which is not an analine dye, is also soluble in spirit. It has a somewhat delayed action, so has to be used with care, but is extremely useful as it tends to tone down red shades, reducing their richness which, of course, is not desirable when staining wood.

As with water colours and fumes, spirit colours may be mixed together to achieve the desired shade and, of course, always test the stain on an unobtrusive part of the piece of furniture before slapping it all over the top surfaces.

If you do not want to mix your own spirit colours a wide range of ready mixed spirit stains is available from most Do-it-yourself shops and colour merchants. These are sold under such names as Yellow Oak, Light Oak, Medium Oak, Dark Oak, Walnut, Rosewood, Brown Mahogany, Teak, etc. These titles, although reasonably descriptive, are misleading as you do not have to use, say, Medium Oak to stain oak, or Brown Mahogany to stain mahogany. Any colour can be used on any wood to achieve the desired effect. Be careful when you buy ready mixed stains that they do not contain any varnish, or other sealing agent. These are usually sold as varnish stains. An enquiry to the colour merchants' salesman will ensure that you get the right kind of stain.

By far the best method is to start off with a very light colour, say yellow oak, and build up your desired colour with successive applications of increasingly darker stains containing those tones which you wish to appear in the finished wood. At the same time you can put in the desired shading at the corners of drawers and recesses in mouldings and carving to achieve the very desirable variations in colour which go with antique furniture.

It is nearly always best to apply your stains with a cotton wool mop wrapped in a piece of lint free cotton material. This avoids leaving telltale brush marks and ensures an even distribution of the stain over all the surfaces to be covered.

Occasionally, particularly with some woods such as oak, you may have difficulty in achieving penetration with the stains. When you encounter this difficulty, you can usually arrive at the desired colour by grinding the colour into the wood by using fine wet and dry carburundum paper or ordinary fine garnet paper while it is still wet. Any surplus stain can be wiped off when the desired tone has been obtained.

Fortunately some woods, particularly Holly, Tulip wood and other exotic woods used for the making of inlays and stringing are almost completely impervious to stains of all kinds, so where inlaid furniture has to be recoloured, you need not fear spoiling the effect by applying stains.

It is, of course, important to know what colour a piece of furniture is going to be after it has been French polished or wax finished. The way that you can do this is to wipe some methylated spirit over the surface. This will show you almost the exact shade and tone of the finished piece and will of course dry out in a minute or so without altering the colour of the wood. There is a third type of wood stain available on the market, sold by Furniglas Ltd., 136–138 Great North Road, Hatfield, Herts. These combine the virtues of both water based and spirit based stains as they are dispersions of extremely finely divided pigments in a mixture of water and alcohol. They also contain other solvents to achieve maximum penetration giving a result similar to the traditional soluble wood dyes.

They are particularly useful when strong coloration is required on impervious or colour resistant timbers, and achieve excellent transparency, enhancement of the grain and contrast in the figuring. Furniglas Fadeless Wood Dyes are obtainable in twelve shades covering the main woods used in furniture manufacture. They can be mixed together to produce the more subtle intermediate tones and can be diluted with water when it is desirable to reduce the intensity of colour.

The process of staining is one of the most subtle operations of furniture restoration. It is an art which can only be learned by experience and practice makes perfect. The first requirement is to achieve even coverage over the whole surface and this requires methodical working by starting at the far edge and covering the area in such a way that no blank areas are left and only the leading edge of the stain is kept wet as it is continually extended until the whole area is evenly coated.

Flat surfaces are best coloured with a piece of rag containing a wad of cotton wool. Carving, quirks and mouldings should be brush coated, the surplus stain being wiped away with a soft clean cloth.

After staining, the article should be set aside so that air can circulate around it.

When you wish to imitate a worn or faded surface, a combination of wiping away some of the stain before it has dried, and sandpapering down after drying, will achieve the desired effect. Great care has to be exercised, however, to avoid leaving hard edges and practice at shading out will be needed.

As a general rule the less stain you use on Antique furniture the better. In many cases the best effect is obtained by using no stain at all, and the best furniture is often so rich in colour contrast and grain figuration that only polishing is required to produce a delightful and mellow finish.

After the application of stains to a surface, it may be found necessary to fade artificially the colours to match the remainder of the piece of furniture. This may be done in a number of ways.

The most delicate effect can be obtained with Hydrogen Peroxide. The alternative is Oxalic Acid solution. If a solution of Oxalic Acid is made with warm water, quite rapid and extensive fading will be achieved. For slight fading make the solution with Methylated Spirits (Oxalic Acid will dissolve in either).

Do not apply the fading agent equally all over the surface, but try to achieve a variation with the maximum fading where handling, polishing and maximum exposure to light and wear would have occurred. The colour should shade to deeper tones in corners and the more inaccessible areas.

After applying the solution, allow twelve hours to dry. All surfaces which have been faded should be washed thoroughly with water and then dried off with a sponge or soft cloth, care being taken that, where veneered surfaces are treated, the veneers do not lift or blister.

From time to time you will have to match up the grain configuration where a repair has necessitated the letting in of a piece of new wood. Of course you will have chosen as close a match to the existing surface for your repair as you can find, but it is next to impossible to find a piece of timber that matches exactly the variations in colour caused by the annual growth lines and grain markings. It is best, therefore, to choose a piece of wood for your repair that has as few lines as possible showing, but conforms in general background texture to the rest of the piece to be repaired.

Once you have balanced up the background colours to match by staining with water or oil stains, the lines of the grain can be painted in using pigment colours. You need to have a good range of pigments in powder form. These can be obtained from any good art shop and are best applied mixed in with Japan Lacquer or Gold Size (also from art shops). Having mixed the correct shades, the grain lines, knots and faults in the wood can be painted in. In a gold size medium they will dry in a few hours and polishing can be commenced in the normal way. Once covered with two or three layers of French Polish, the repair will be almost completely invisible if the grain has been imitated skilfully.

The skilful use of stains is an art that can only be acquired with practice. The more staining and tinting that you do, the more skilled you become, but as your skill increases you will be spurred on to try more daring experiments. Straightforward staining is extremely simple and fortunately you can always remove recently applied stains with Oxalic Acid or other bleaching agents and start again.

The more you experiment the more adventurous you will become and the more pleased you will be at your achievements. So do spare as much time as you can on perfecting your knowledge of colouring wood. The final appearance of any piece of furniture hinges on the staining stage more than on any other step of the finishing, so it is well worth while mastering this art as, once the skill is acquired, immense satisfaction will be the reward.

Chapter 12

FILLING GRAIN AND STOPPING CRACKS
When antique or old furniture has been stripped, it is unlikely that the surface of any wood will need filling before repolishing. If repairs have been made, however, the surfaces of all freshly cut or new wood will have to be 'filled'.

The pores or cells of all wood fibre, to a varying degree, appear as a pattern of small indentations or craters which, if left unfilled, show up as an uneven surface as soon as polish is applied to the surface. As an even surface is normally required, these pores in the grain have to be filled.

Two kinds of filler are available and either one can be used with equal success. Both types are available under a variety of proprietary labels. There is no advantage in making up your own fillers, as the proprietary ones are extremely effective and easy to use. One type is in the form of a paste or slurry mixture of silica ground with linseed oil, Japan dryer, white spirit and various coloured pigments. Some fillers have to be broken down to a thin cream with white spirit before application; others are ready to use straight from the container and in all cases the colour can be adjusted by the addition of spirit or oil stains.

Care should be taken before application to ensure that the colour blends with the background colour of the wood as subsequent colouring is difficult, and alteration of the colour of the wood is bound to result. Sometimes you see furniture covered with light flecks where the grain filler has not been suitably coloured before application. Until a few years ago plaster of Paris or mixtures of whiting and plaster were used for filling and these are particularly prone to colour fading.

The prepared paste filler is rubbed vigorously *across* the grain to ensure penetration into the grain, using a coarse rag or stiff brush, such as a boot brush or natural *bristle* tooth brush and finished off with a light stroke in the direction of the grain. The surface is now left to dry for about 4–8 hours and the whole surface is then sanded down with fairly fine glass or garnet paper; with open grain woods a second application may be necessary.

The second type of fillers are known as liquid wood fillers which need agitation before use and frequent stirring to keep the filling agents in suspension. The liquid vehicle in which the filler is carried is normally a thin solution of Shelac in spirit. These fillers are applied with a brush and, as they dry rapidly, should be spread thoroughly with short strokes, maintaining a wet edge to the work. Several applications are required to fill open grain woods and light rubbing down with glass paper after each coat, or every other coat if the grain is particularly open in character, is necessary. Continue applying coats of filler until it can be seen that the grain has been completely filled to the degree required. Again, these liquid fillers can be tinted with stain if this is required. This type of filler is particularly useful on close grain woods, such as Cuban mahogany when only one or two coats will be required.

The filling and concealment of cracks and joints presents a series of different problems and there are a variety of materials available. The choice of the right material to use depends largely on the effect required, the age of the piece of furniture and the skill of the user.

First of all, with very old oak furniture, large holes and cracks can be very satisfactorily filled with a mixture of oak sawdust and Scotch Glue Size. This mixture is prepared by damping a quantity of fine sawdust with water until it just holds together when squeezed in the hand. At this stage the colour can be adjusted with water based stains, particularly vandyke crystals with the addition of tumeric and, if

94

necessary, pigment colours. There must be no excess of moisture and the hand should remain dry after squeezing. To this mixture add ordinary carpenters glue from the gluepot which has been thinned down with warm water to Size; about three parts of water to one of glue. Mix thoroughly in a suitable tin or bowl to a dry squeeze consistency. When you make a ball in your hand and squeeze it, no moisture can be extracted. This mixture applied with a spatula or chisel scraper and forced into the crack or hole can, when dry, be worked in the same way as wood, it can be sanded down and will even hold a screw securely if necessary. Quite large areas can be filled in with the mixture and it can be stained in the normal way.

On later furniture, particularly that of the walnut period, where large cracks often appear due to the shrinkage of the carcase wood, causing splits in veneered surfaces, it is best to use a hard wax filler. This furniture is so valuable and usually of such good colour and patina that any disturbance of the surface will do irreparable damage and complete conceal-ment of cracks is neither desirable or recommended as the result will only be a reduction in both the charm and the value of a piece of furniture of such age and rarity.

Hard filling waxes can be obtained in a variety of colours and are similar to ordinary sealing wax. The best method of application is to heat up the tang of a file, or similar steel pointed tool and melt the stick of wax holding it on the hot metal. The melted wax will run down the tang and can be directed into the crack. After hardening off, but before com-pletely cold, all excess wax can be trimmed off with a sharp chisel. The surface can then be polished over with beeswax.

For a general filler on most furniture, Brummer stopper is the best material to use. This is obtainable in a wide range of shades from white and cream, through the browns and red-browns to black. A range of these should be kept in the workshop. They are in the form of a hard paste which can easily be introduced into cracks and holes with a narrow chisel scraper. They have the great advantage that no shrinkage takes place when they harden off and, normally, hardening will only take an hour or so.

They can be used to stop almost any small gap from a worm hole to a joint or crack and will stain down to colour with most normal stains. A good tip is to mix two appropriate colours roughly together to produce a marble effect. This will add to the degree of concealment to the crack. They are not, however, particularly satisfactory for filling long wide cracks in table tops or other plane surfaces as concealment in these circumstances is well nigh impossible. This kind of fault has to be concealed by the splicing in of a slip of matching wood.

If you do not use the stopper regularly, you may find that the contents of a partly used tin hardens off—particularly if the lid is not firmly replaced. It can be reconstituted by the addition of a few drops of water, providing it has not become rock hard.

Remember always, stoppers are only to be used with great moderation. They are not a suitable alternative to accurate workmanship and if used to cover up sloppy work or mistakes, the results will be obvious and disappointing. Used sensibly they are a great aid to securing a superb result but they should always be invisible when the job is completed. There is always a temptation to use them to cut corners and save time, but this temptation must be resisted.

Chapter 13

FRENCH POLISHING

There is a vast difference between repolishing a piece of antique furniture that has recently been stripped and polishing from scratch a new piece of furniture that has just been constructed from new raw wood.

Fortunately, you will be principally concerned with repolishing old wood that, in spite of stripping, is more or less prepared to receive a French polish finish. To begin with, the wood has already been filled and the surface levelled, the grain has been consolidated and time has ensured that the whole piece of furniture is in a relatively stable state.

The very process of stripping and the cleaning down with wire wool has helped further to burnish the surface and compress the grain and, with any luck, a considerable degree of the original patination remains. It is only where repairs involving the splicing in of newly cut wood have been done that additional filling and sealing processes will have to be undertaken.

French polishing is a skilled craft, involving the understanding of the effects and application of a large variety of materials. A skilled French polisher can produce a vast variety of effects on a piece of furniture but this does not mean that a complete novice may not, with no more than a few hours practice, produce extremely pleasing and quite professional results.

A generation or so ago our Victorian and Edwardian ancestors favoured having their furniture very highly polished to what is known as a piano finish. In other words, dozens and dozens of coats of French polish were applied to the surfaces of the wood, many of them containing red and purple stains, to produce a finish that looked like a skating rink that had just been scraped flat and brushed spotlessly clean.

The combination of layers of polish and colouring materials, to a great extent, obscure the beauty and natural grain configurations of the timber, producing an effect which is totally unacceptable to modern tastes. Today, in fact, the finish that is generally accepted as being most pleasing, is one that shows the natural beauty of the timber, preferably, in mahogany furniture, having a 'hay' or 'honey' colour; allowing to some degree the grain of the wood to show through and having a mellow, not too shiny but deep waxed texture. It is a method of achieving this finish that I am first going to describe, leaving until later a discussion of the finer details of the craft of French polishing.

This course has been chosen in order to encourage you to take the plunge and not be frightened or over-awed at the task of French polishing. Rest assured that this process is not as difficult or complicated as you may, up to now, have been led to believe. Due to the availability of new and very cleverly formulated materials, professional results can be achieved by the novice French polisher, and experience has shown that women can easily become just as proficient as men in this branch of restoration as they can at all of the other skills involved in the renovation of antique furniture.

Remember Confucius who said: 'The longest of journeys starts with a single step'.

The product with which you should start on your French polishing career is Furniglas Home French Polish. This is available in a 'do it yourself' pack containing two liquids, Furniglas No. 1 which is a specially formulated French polish and Furniglas No. 2 which is a finishing, buffing and hardening medium. These two, used in conjunction, will produce, with the minimum of snags, exactly the result which is most desirable by today's standards and, at the same time, will produce a surface which is more durable and resistant to stains, ring marks and other blemishes than the traditional French polished surfaces.

Two shades of Furniglas French Polish are available: both are translucent; the standard polish imparts a pale amber tint and enriches dark woods: the white French Polish is practically colourless and is used on very light and delicate woods where the minimum of colour variation is desirable.

Furniglas also produce a newer Polyurethane version of their home French polish which is even more resistant to surface damage than the original, and is ideal for dining and dressing tables and other pieces of furniture likely to be subjected to heavy wear and tear. This is slightly more difficult to apply, so for your first experiment stick to the original Furniglas Home French Polish.

First of all you should assemble all of the things that you are going to require as follows:

(a) A few sheets of 9/0 Garnet Finishing paper or Lubrisil non clog paper. Grades 320 (fine) and 180. Garnet paper is far better and more economical than ordinary fine glass paper. It lasts longer and does not pick up and retain particles of the polish so readily. Lubrisil is even better, as it incorporates a dry lubricant with the abrasive and is even more resistant to clogging than Garnet paper.

(b) Cotton wool. 1 lb. rolls of non-medicated wool can be bought from almost any chemist.

(c) A supply of clean, soft, fluff-free cotton rags. Old handkerchiefs or worn thin bed sheets are ideal.

(d) Clean yellow dusters.

(e) Methylated spirit.

(f) A couple of old jam jars, complete with tight fitting lids.

(g) A cork sanding block.

Before starting, examine the piece of furniture to be polished very carefully. Dust it over to make sure that it is entirely free from dust, grit or any other unwanted dirt and is entirely free from oil or grease. Remember, perfection depends on an even foundation. If you find that any holes or blemishes have been overlooked, attend to them before you start polishing.

Make sure that the room in which you are working is warm (at least above 60°F. 16°C) and is dust free. In cold temperatures French polish tends to bloom and turns milky on the surfaces you have polished. Dust is the great enemy of the French polisher.

Before starting polishing it is wise to protect your hands with an application of Rozalex or other suitable barrier cream. Alternatively thin polythene surgical gloves can be worn. Thick rubber gloves are not recommended as they reduce the feeling that you require in your finger tips. When you have finished polishing, your hands should be cleaned up with a cotton wool swab wetted with methylated spirit. Working continuously over the hands is more effective than concentrating on one finger at a time.

Next make a polishing pad but cutting out a square of cotton wool about 7″ × 7″. Fold it in half diagonally to make a triangle and then fold each corner in to the centre, in the same way as you fold a baby's nappy.

This cotton pad is now enveloped in a piece of cotton rag 8–9″ square. The surplus on the sides and corners of the rag is given a twist and retained in the palm of your hand. Your fingers are extended and the pad is gripped lightly by the finger tips. Practice this before you apply the polish to the pad, or fad as it is often termed.

The cotton wool acts as a reservoir for the French polish (Furniglas No. 1), the rag holds the fad together and ensures that you deposit no fluff on the surface when polishing. By increasing or decreasing the pressure of your finger tips you regulate the flow of the polish.

Now remove the cloth from the cotton wool, dip the rag in the methylated spirit and wring it out. Open out the cotton wool to a triangle, place it on the flat rag in the palm of your hand and wet the cotton wool with French polish. Fold in the corners and screw the pad up as previously described.

The general principles of French polishing are as follows:

(a) Build up an even coating of polish on the surface by repeated and fairly generous applications of polish, followed by sanding down lightly with abrasives.

(b) Perfecting the final surface by long strokes with a relatively dry pad.

(c) Burnishing and hardening the surface with Furniglas No. 2.

You start off by the process known as 'bodying in' by methodically applying the polish to the surface in a series of tight circular movements. Start at the top left-hand corner furthest away from where you are standing and move your pad progressively to the right so that each circular motion half overlaps the previous one, thus completely covering the surface with a film of polish. When you get to the right hand edge, pull your hand towards you slightly and proceed in the opposite direction, slightly overlapping the first row of spirals. Continue in a similar manner, backwards and

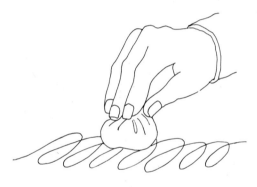

The French polishing pad

forwards until the entire surface is covered. You must be extremely careful that you do not leave any blobs of excess polish behind as these will tear up the surface already laid down when you return for the next coat. If you go back immediately and pick up any surplus polish no harm will be done. As you progress in building up the coats of polish it is, of course, increasingly important not to leave any blobs behind. Remember, you control the flow of the polish by finger-tip pressure on the pad.

You will find that polish is squeezed through the pad very

easily when it is new, more slowly with progressive use. At first your pad will require recharging at quite frequent intervals, as it grows older it will become less resilient and eventually the cotton wool will have to be discarded. When you recharge, apply the polish to the centre of the cotton wool, never apply polish directly on to the rag. The covering rag will also become clogged with polish, so keep a spare one soaking in meths and change over from time to time, wring out thoroughly each time before re-use.

You will find that the surface of the polish dries in a few seconds, but do not keep on going over the same area repeatedly, make sure that your strokes progress steadily along the work. As your arm gets tired you can vary the stroke on later coats by using a figure of eight movement.

After you have applied 10–12 coats let the work stand for a short while to harden off and then sand over lightly with garnet or lubrisil paper.

On some open-grained timbers, the whole process may have to be repeated to achieve a satisfactory foundation. Always sand down after about twelve coats and continue until you are satisfied with the surface filling and levelling out of blemishes. When sanding down, only the surface has to be levelled, do not remove any more than a small proportion of the polish.

Now you come to Stage (B). With a dryer and firmer pad which will leave no wet patches or ridges of polish start polishing with long graceful strokes of even weight. Vary the position where the pad comes into contact with the surface every time and continue the stroke beyond the end of the work. Wherever possible polish in the same direction as the grain. Again, at least twelve complete coverings are required. No further sandings should be necessary, and if you place the work in a position to allow the light to strike obliquely across the surface, you can observe that you have achieved a satisfactory surface without faults, specks, or other blemishes.

Once you are satisfied, set the work aside for at least three hours and then polish again until the pad dries up. In order to keep your polishing pads from drying out, keep them in a tightly closed jam jar. They can be kept in this way for several weeks without deterioration. Old compacted pads are useful for several processes.

Set the work aside again for a minimum of two hours and you are ready for Stage (C). For this you use Furniglas No. 2, preferably within twenty-four hours of your completing Stage (B), using only a pad for new cotton wool. The pad is first generously wetted with the liquid which must first be well shaken up to suspend the burnishing agents. Polish one manageable strip at a time, and exerting pressure rub with the grain at least twenty times. While the section is still moist, polish with a clean dry duster, this time with swifter, lighter strokes until the surface is dry and shining brilliantly. The same process is repeated until the entire piece of furniture is completed.

You will find that the surface of the cotton wool becomes felted and coated with a film of polish. This should be peeled off at fairly frequent intervals. If you keep the pad flat and do not screw it up into a ball this is easy to do, and new layers of cotton wool can be added to the dry side of the pad.

Be careful not to spill Furniglas No. 2 on to carpets, clothes, etc. If you do have a mishap, wash out at once with soap or soda and warm water.

The above are the basic instructions for using Furniglas French polish. Once you have mastered these basic skills and convinced yourself that you can produce a level, blemish-free, surface on a piece of furniture you can start to experiment with the slightly more complicated variations. The confidence which you have acquired to repolish any surface provides you with a licence to try other things, secure in the knowledge that, if you make any mistakes, you can strip it all off and re-finish the whole area.

In the chapter on Cleaning, Reviving and Stripping, we touched on water stains, light scratches, white discolorations, alcohol rings and heat marks, in French polished surfaces. By running your finger tips over the discoloured or marked surface you can feel if there is any unevenness. If none can be felt, it is likely that a thorough burnishing with Furniglas No. 2, or any of the other recommended revivers will obliterate the damage. When this treatment fails the next step is to sand down the area until smooth with Garnet 9/0 or Lubrisil 320 paper. Try to avoid removal of the colour, creating a pale patch, but if this is unavoidable, correct the colour by the addition of spirit stains to the French polish. These can be added direct to the polishing pad but here a word of warning—make sure that you do not add too much colour at first: the colour can be built up with successive coats of French polish.

Before starting to French polish any patch, you must dewax the surface. This is best done with white spirit on a coarse rag or on a ball of fine wire wool. Under no circumstances attempt to dewax with methylated spirit, or you will lift the existing French polish.

When polishing in patches you should confine the applications of French polish to the patch at first. When you have built up the level to that of the existing finish, sand down the whole area and repolish with two or three applications of the rubber. Finally, Furniglas No. 2 can be used to fuse the new into the old polish, completely concealing the new patch.

Where you encounter deeper scratches, to speed up the process of levelling off the polish, expose a small quantity of Furniglas No. 1 in a bottle cap, or similar suitable receptacle, until it is rather treacly. Use a pointed match stick to apply the thickened polish exactly into the scratch and leave until hardened. Then sand down and polish in the same way as dealing with discolorations and light scratches.

If the scratches are so deep that the wood shows up as a lighter colour, before filling the wound with thickened polish, apply a little stain, or add stain to the polish to bring it to a suitable colour.

Dealing with cigarette burns, deep holes or chips in veneers calls for a little more drastic treatment. First the area has to be prepared by cutting away all discoloration, charred wood, or rust stained areas to ensure that the repair will not be 'framed' by a dark surround. No matter how proud you are of your repair work, the last thing you want is for it to stick out like a sore thumb.

Edges of the area for repair should be slightly undercut to give the stopper a slight purchase to hold it firmly in place.

Where a bold figure runs through the repair area, cut a V nick into the edge of the good wood to break the line of the join where it runs across the grain. Always try to avoid straight lines, except when cutting along the grain of straight-grained woods. A curved line is more difficult for the eye to follow and it helps to conceal the finished repair.

Carefully clean out all old glue, dust and other debris. Next, with an artist's fine brush coat the upper inside edges of the hole with Furniglas No. 1. This prevents the exposed end grain from taking up any stain and showing as a dark surround to the repair.

With a small chisel scraper or putty knife, firmly press Brummer stopper or plastic wood firmly into the cavity, making sure that it bites firmly on to the undercut edges, leaving it finally slightly proud of the surface. Deep holes, such as nail or screw cavities, should be packed with match sticks or slips of wood, terminating below the surface to speed up the hardening of the stopper. The deeper the cavity, the longer the stopper will take to harden.

The stopper used should be slightly lighter in colour than the general shade of the wood. If you examine most woods, you will find that they are made up of a multiplicity of colours and, ideally, your stopper should be the colour of the lightest element in the grain of the timber being patched.

If there are several repairs in close proximity on any one surface, it is best to block sand the whole area in the normal way. If a single repair has to be levelled, care is required to avoid making a shallow local depression or creating a pale patch. If you fold back a corner or end of a narrow strip of garnet paper, to make an abrasive pad, with the tip of one finger you can rotate the abrasive area on the stopping, avoiding contact with neighbouring surfaces. Finally sand off with fine paper on a small block of wood to bring the repair finally to uniform height with the surface.

Next, scratch out with a darning needle an imitation of the grain channels, joining up with the adjacent indentations, following precisely their direction and vary their length.

An exact match of colour is not always easy to achieve, so a little practice with various strengths and shades of stain on a test piece of stopper is advisable. Use a fine water-colour artist's brush and several shades of stain to copy the variation in grain colours and follow the general grain configuration.

When you are satisfied that you have found the right colours on the test piece, apply them to the repair, brushing inwards from the edges of the stopping and following the direction of the grain.

It is sometimes effective and easier to turn repairs of this kind into natural-looking knots. The minimum of artistic talent is required and the result will certainly conceal small repairs completely.

As you gain confidence with your French polishing, you will be able to tackle patch polishing, where there is local damage (such as a ring from the bottom of a glass) without stripping the whole surface. First sand down the damaged area with garnet paper. The area sanded should not be *smaller* than 5″ × 5″ and, while doing so, take note of the colour of the dust on the paper. If it is white, use Furniglas White Home French Polish; if it is slightly buff coloured, use Standard Furniglas Home French Polish. The use of a 'white' French polish, particularly on very light woods, like Satinwood or blond mahogany, is always advised, as the 'Standard' or brown coloured French polish tends to tint the wood.

Apply twelve or more coverings with a very small pad, making slight and varying overlaps on to the surrounding surface. Where the original polish was fairly thick, a repeat application may be necessary. When the new surface is at the same level as the original polish, Furniglas No. 2 should be applied vigorously in the normal manner to fuse the new and the old surfaces into one uniform and perfect finish.

If any outlines of the repaired area show, it may be advisable to sand over the whole area and skim the whole surface with polish.

When sanding down any surface, sand with the direction of the grain, by this means you avoid leaving visible scratches on the surface of your work. Avoid like the plague any type of rotating tool, either for sanding or polishing, as this will invariably leave a series of circular marks which are the very devil to remove. If you must use a mechanical device, orbital sanders are acceptable for all but final rubbing down, and belt sanders are also suitable in the majority of cases.

Where you have made a repair with new wood or veneer, or have a bare patch of wood to be polished, this procedure should be followed: First sand the patch and near surrounding polish with 6/o Garnet paper (or 'o' glasspaper) and then colour in the new wood to match. The main colouring of the wood is applied before filling the grain and polishing. At least two hours should elapse between staining and applying polish. Complete the match in with successive *brush coats* of tinted Furniglas No. 1.

By using tinted French polish, you can achieve a perfect blend in with the existing surface, and applying French polish with a brush speeds up the process of filling up the grain. When you are satisfied with the surface and the colour, change over to a small pad and to untinted French polish. Sand down lightly and finish as previously described.

Where an inlaid piece of furniture has been stripped and recolouring of the background surface is required without altering the colour or darkening the inlays; an accurately applied coat of white French polish over the inlays is recommended. For safety's sake, apply two coats to ensure that no areas of inlay are missed, and leave for twelve hours before applying the stain. Wipe off all residues of the stain with a dry absorbent rag, wiping in the direction of the grain. When thoroughly dry, apply one brush coat of French polish and then continue polishing in the normal manner.

Finally, a word of warning—newly polished surfaces take a few days to harden off completely, so do not use newly polished articles for a few days. After about two weeks a further treatment of Furniglas No. 2 is recommended to complete the burnishing and hardening of the surface.

You have now produced a 'bright' highly reflective finish which is not entirely acceptable on antique furniture. What is normally required is a deep polished and waxed satin effect. This is achieved by rubbing down the fully hardened surface with fine steel wool—Grade 000 or 0000. Always rub with the grain and frequently clean out the polish residues from the surface of the steel wool pad. The piece of furniture is now ready for wax polishing.

So far, all the instructions on French polishing have related to a proprietary brand which experience has shown to be straightforward in application and extremely durable. At this stage a few words on traditional and less sophisticated French polishes may be helpful or of interest.

French polish is basically a solution of shelac resin in methylated spirit and, until a few years ago, most French polishers made up their own from flake shelacs. Today you can buy French polish solutions in a variety of shades and qualities as follows:

Transparent Polish is a nearly colourless liquid which is used on light woods to retain the natural colour as far as possible.

White Polish is a slightly opaque polish which is sometimes used on white woods to brighten their appearance. It should never be used on dark timber.

Button Polish has a yellow tint and is sometimes used as a base to neutralise mahogany which is too red. It is slightly opaque and unsuitable for use on dark timbers.

Garnet Polish is a dark brown translucent polish, normally used for the polishing of dark coloured timbers.

Black or Ebony Polish is a material used for producing an ebonised finish, particularly favoured at the end of the 18th Century during the Classical and Egyptian period when heavily brass inlaid ebonised furniture was much in fashion.

Table Top Polishes are designed to be resistant to heat and water marks and are claimed to be light resistant as well. They are usually based on cellulose.

Polyurethane Polishes are newer polishes which are applied in the same way as shelac based polishes, but take longer to dry between coats. They have great toughness and resistance to boiling water, dilute acids, spirits and scratching. The solvent base is cellulose thinners not methylated spirits. They are slightly more difficult to use than traditional shelac polishes.

Piano Polishes are heavier shelac polishes, containing a higher proportion of resins and are designed to produce 'polished glass' surfaces.

Brush Polishes are designed for application with a soft paint or varnish brush and to flow out to an even surface.

Coloured Polishes are made by adding spirit soluble analine dyes to light coloured or transparent polishes to produce the required tint in the finished piece of furniture.

The traditional techniques of the French Polisher are many and varied, every exponent of the craft having his own methods and secrets. A long apprenticeship was normal and today very few expert craftsmen can be found.

Assuming that the process is starting from scratch on a new piece of furniture that has been rubbed down and fully prepared, the first process is to fill the grain. This is done by applying a number of coats of a liquid filler, such as Gedges Duraxcote, alternatively, with close-grained timbers a brush coat of French polish may be applied. A special brushing technique, unlike the application of paint, is required. The polish dries so rapidly that very careful application with a soft brush, known as a mop, charged with very little polish, is employed. The polish is laid on with short strokes and no attempt is made to brush out the polish after application. Care must be taken to leave no access polish in corners or carved areas, and the flow of the polish is controlled by the pressure of the brush. This technique is essential for the polishing of carvings and deep mouldings.

Several progressive techniques are used for polishing with a pad. Possibly the best for the initial process is that known as scrubbing in or grinding in. For this an old well compacted pad of cotton wool is employed, wrapped in a coarse cloth. A piece of thin canvas is ideal. French polish, diluted in 5–10 volumes of methylated spirit is used, the pad being only slighted wetted. The scrubbing in is done with spiral or figure-of-eight motions as previously described. Only after eight to a dozen coats will a discernible sheen develop. As soon as this happens, the interior surface of the rubber is dusted lightly with very fine pumice, jeweller's rouge or fine rottenstone. The combination of a fine abrasive and the thin polish produces a thin, hard and durable surface, ideal for either wax polishing or as a basis for a full French polished finish.

Skimming-in is a variation sometimes used, but not much recommended as there is a danger of producing too soft a polish. A drop of raw linseed oil (not boiled) is added to the rubber. In this case the polish is not diluted, but this addition of oil aids the penetration of the polish into the surface and, at the same time, prevents the rubber from sticking to the newly polished surface. As little oil as possible is used and as much pressure as can be exerted while polishing in tight spirals across the surface.

The next process after either scrubbing or skimming-in is that of Bodying-up. This is, in effect, a continuation with normal strength polish of the process of building up a hard film of polish on the surface of the wood—a softer, more springy rubber is used during this stage and great care has to be taken in controlling the flow of the polish and ensuring that an even coating is applied to the surface. The size of the spiral is increased, and from time to time the whole surface is polished out with straight sweeps in the direction of the grain from one extremity of the work to the other without halting or lifting the rubber.

The final process is 'spiriting off' and is done after the work has been allowed to settle for a few hours, preferably overnight. Here again, a well used and compacted rubber is used which is moistened with a half and half mixture of polish and methylated spirit. Only straight strokes with the rubber are employed and great care has to be taken that the rubber does not stop for an instant on any part of the surface. Towards the end of this process the rubber is allowed to dry out progressively and the pressure exerted is increased. This will produce a diamond hard glass-like surface. Some polishers again use a tiny drop of raw linseed oil during this process, but this tends to leave smears on the surface that have to be removed next day with a soft cloth very slightly moistened with a mixture of water and methylated spirit or, alternatively, a liquid furniture polish.

Chapter 14

WAX POLISHING

The ideal surface for all oak, elm and fruitwood furniture is a deep, wax polish. Present fashion also dictates that walnut and mahogany furniture should have the 'wax polish' look. This does not necessarily mean, however, that, when repolishing, only wax finishings should be used to produce the desired effect.

Certainly wax polishing with beeswax and wood turpentine can be achieved, but only at the cost of great physical effort over a considerable period. A method has been developed to produce a short cut to a beeswax high polish and for those of you who are determined to achieve this, details are given later on in this chapter. However, the same effect can be produced much more easily by starting off with a sealing coat of shelac on which a coat of wax polish can be built up quickly.

Again, when considering the question of which wax polish to use, it is possible, and the work of only half-an-hour, to make your own wax polish. Sheratons receipt for polishing wax is given below. Even simpler, shred up a jar full of beeswax lightly packed down. Add to it enough real turpentine to reach the level of the wax. Put in as much carbon black as you can pile on a new penny piece and heat in a saucepan of water over a low flame. When melted, stir well and allow to set to a soft mass of the consistency of lard.

On the other hand, a number of manufacturers have spent

many years in research to produce excellent polishes which work well and shine up quickly. Particularly to be recommended are the Durax range made by Gedges, and the Harracks and Briwax ranges made by Henry Flack, available only from them. In many antique shops you can also buy Antiquax or Sheradale. All these waxes are produced in a variety of colours from clear white to very dark jacobean

It is extremely useful to have a range of colours available as the final tone and shading can be given to any piece of furniture by their use. Brown and stain waxes are particularly useful on all but the lightest of furniture woods as they impart the very mellowness to newly renovated pieces that is the essence of a well cared for antique.

In most cases, the current practice for final finishing is to apply a few coats of French polish to the surfaces of the piece of furniture under treatment. Use either the Furniglas method, limiting the number of coats to the degree of grain filling required and finishing with Furniglas No. 2, and then dulling the surface with fine wire wool to provide a key for the wax or using the scrubbing in technique, finishing with fine pumice.

The wax polish should now be liberally applied with an old, short haired paint brush, or a shoe brush. The wax should be well scrubbed in, first against the grain then finally, more lightly, in the direction of the grain. Cover the whole area of the piece of furniture, excluding, of course, the back and bottom sides which are not normally polished. A varying amount of time, depending on the brand of polish used, must be allowed to elapse to allow some of the solvents to evaporate.

The next stage is to polish in vigorously with a soft cloth. Mutton cloth is an ideal thing to use, and can be purchased in rolls from most hardware shops. As the shine begins to appear, change over to a clean cloth and polish entirely in the direction of the grain.

It must be understood that wax polishing a piece of furniture is an operation which should be done thoroughly. Don't be stingy with the polish during the first waxing and be prepared to spend at least an hour on the average size piece, such as a chest of drawers. Waxing is best done before the handles are replaced, but the best way of keeping handles free from oxydisation is to give them also a polish over with clear white wax. This will keep them bright without unattractive glazed look that you get if they are lacquered.

Most people these days seem to like their brass fittings bright, but not so bright that they look brand new. If you do not have a buffing wheel, brass handles can be cleaned satisfactorily with steel wool and Brasso. If they are badly corroded, they can be cleaned up with an overnight soak, completely covered by a solution of Horolene made by Horological Solvents Ltd., Bury, Lancs. You should be able to get it from your nearest clock and watch repairer.

For those who wish to produce an entirely wax finish on raw unsealed wood, the technique is to use a beeswax and turpentine polish and to apply it in the same way as for French polishing. The pad which you use, however, is made entirely from a soft cotton square, folded very carefully into a sausage shape. Turn the ends in and grip the pad firmly along the length of the palm, retaining it with the thumb on one side and the fingers on the other. This pad should be wetted with methylated spirits and kept moist with spirit during the polishing process. The best way to do this is to keep the meths in an oil can, so that the amount of spirit added to the pad can be controlled. Only enough spirit to damp the rag must be used and it must be kept just moist to the touch.

The principle is that the meths melts the wax and allows it to flow. If too much is used, the wax crystallizes out, leaving an opaque film on the surface which destroys the beauty of the timber below. Very vigorous rubbing is called for and the process is rather tedious, although the results are most attractive.

An alternative is to use Gedges No. 7 Wax or Henry Flacks' Briwax, both of which are specially formulated for use on unsealed wood. When using these, no meths is required as they contain their own special solvents to prevent crystallization.

Once a piece of furniture, either sealed or unsealed, has

been thoroughly wax polished,* it only requires burnishing with a clean duster once every week or so. A light application of any good wax polish should be applied about once every three to four months.

The only kind of polish you should avoid using on antique furniture is that containing Silicones. Good as silicones are for repelling dust and liquids, they produce an impervious seal on the surface of the wood so that it cannot feed on the waxes and oils which polishes contain, and which are beneficial to the continued wellbeing of your furniture.

Persevere with the wax polishing of your furniture, the longer they are tended the deeper and mellower will the surface become and in the fullness of time they will bear a patina which will be your pride and joy.

*Sheraton's recipe for a polishing wax

'. . . take beeswax and a small quantity of turpentine in a clean earthen pan, and set it over a fire till the wax unites with the turpentine, which it will do by constant stirring about; add to this a little red lead finely ground upon a stone, together with a small portion of fine Oxford ochre, to bring the whole to the colour of brisk mahogany.

'Lastly, when you take it off the fire, add a little copal varnish to it, and mix it well together, then turn the whole into a basin of water, and while it is yet warm, work it into a ball, with which the brush is to be rubbed as before observed. And observe, with a ball of wax and brush kept for this purpose entirely, furniture in general may be kept in good order.'

Chapter 15

THE RESTORATION OF LACQUERED AND PAINTED FURNITURE

Lacquered, Japanned or Indian ware, as it has been variously termed, enjoyed its first popular vogue at the time of the restoration of Charles II (1649–75), although examples of original oriental work were imported into England as far back as the time of Elizabeth. It continued to enjoy a varying degree of popularity beyond the middle of the 18th Century, but was particularly in favour in the third quarter of the 17th Century, and again during the 1750's. There was also a revival of the vogue in the early 19th Century. During each period of peak popularity 'amateur' exponents of the craft flourished and, in consequence, a volume of indifferent and downright inferior examples are still to be found mixed in with the most beautiful and well executed work of both professional and amateur craftsmen. The original oriental art of lacquer decoration has been practiced in the East for thousands of years and depends on the availability of the sap of the lac tree, which cannot be preserved in liquid form. European imitators, therefore, had to devise alternative methods and have shown great ingenuity, if not originality, in producing a similar result to this ancient technique of decoration.

It is interesting and useful to note that, while oriental lacquer work was superb, their joinery was generally considered to be slipshod and inferior by English and European standards. In consequence at various times furniture was produced in Europe and sent to the orient for lacquering.

Screens were imported (taking up comparatively little space in ships holds) and the panels used for incorporation in European furniture and both European joiners and oriental lacquerers have been either 'sent out', or 'brought in' to practice their skills. Some work executed in Europe, particularly in what is now Holland, is so near to oriental perfection that it can baffle even the expert in identification.

Two basic kinds of lacquer work from the 17th Century are to be found; Chinese and Japanese incised work, where the designs were cut into 'coromandel' lacquer. This is often known as Bantam work. Secondly the very much more common raised work of gilded and painted features on a plain coloured background, which is more often than not black or red, although examples with green, yellow, even blue backgrounds, are occasionally encountered.

The materials used to build up the background of oriental work are usually of a reddish-brown colour, while those of English and Continental origin invariably grey or white, because the building up compound used in England was a mixture of whiting and glue size applied in a succession of thin coats to a depth of anything up to a quarter of an inch. After the base for the decoration was completed, the surface was appropriately coloured and then varnished. Final decoration was added and the surface was then highly polished.

Victorian work invariably has a black base.

The 'Gesso', which is the name given to the base material, is made by first grinding ordinary whiting to a fine paste with water to remove any trace of lumpy particles. The paste should be the same consistency as thick cream and to this should be added enough scotch glue to reduce it to the texture of a thin pouring cream. Lastly, add a few drops of raw linseed oil (about 3 drops per egg cupful) and mix well.

Broken or missing areas can then be built up again with successive coats of the Gesso to their original height and allowed to dry thoroughly before rubbing down with fine garnet paper to a marble smooth, polished finish. Where original gesso has become detached from the base woodwork due to shrinkage, new gesso can be worked in underneath with a palette knife and cracks can be filled in similarly.

Where large areas are to be restored, the gesso should be scraped down with a square edged steel scraper. This can be ground to shape to fit mouldings. After a time you will build up a set of shaped tools which can be used on almost any shape. At all times the surfaces must be dust free and should be wiped down with a damp cloth. This applies equally to partly completed work as well as to old damaged surfaces.

Once the gesso has been restored and rubbed down, the surface has to be sized with a white pigment base, ground with real turpentine and finally mixed into goldsize. In all cases, grinding can either be done in a small mortar with a pestle, or on a white ceramic tile with a palette knife. The best white pigment to use is Titanium, because it gives better cover. A few spots of blue can be added, to indicate that you have achieved complete cover with your sizeing coat. When this coat is dry, rub down with wire wool.

The new design, as near as you can make it to the original now has to be marked out on the new gesso areas and coloured in to match the general design. It is best to use pigment colours ground with turpentine and mixed into goldsize, as this type of paint dries quickly, but if you are more familiar with the use of oil paints and do not mind waiting for them to dry, these can be used.

Paint on enough coats, rubbing down between each coat, to give you a match. Final toning down can be achieved by blowing or dusting on a very light application of brown, grey or black dry pigment colour when the last coat is almost dry. Then distressing down when completely dry with fine wire wool.

Finally the surface should be 'varnished' over with either a few coats of clear French polish or one of the new synthetic varnishes. An 'antique finish' can be obtained by using slightly tinted French polish.

Where a whole piece of lacquered furniture has lost its lustre, a coat or so of clear French polish will restore it to its former brilliance. First, of course, you must clean all the surfaces thoroughly to remove the old dirt and grime. In most cases white spirit on a cotton swab will achieve this. In some cases you will find that the brilliance of the decoration is achieved by painting translucent colours over gold leaf. In these cases an application of gold leaf has to be made in the appropriate areas. More of this technique later on in the gilding section.

In places where whole areas of, say, a gesso picture frame, or a complete rosette or other decoration, are found to be missing, a new motif must be cast from a composition material. If you can get it, use dental plaster of paris mixed with glue size, if not, ordinary plaster of paris will do.

A mould must first be made from some other part of the decoration which is similar to the missing portion and perfect. This can be done for simple shapes with plasticine or similar modelling material, but the best mould making compound is Vinamould which you can buy from Alec Tiranti Ltd. of 70 High St., Theale, Berks.

Vinamould has to be melted in a tin or old saucepan and poured over the feature from which you wish to make a mould. Obviously, in order to contain the liquid Vinamould, you have to construct a dam on some occasions. This can be done with pieces of softwood, held down temporarily with a couple of veneer pins. The area from which the cast is to be taken must be oiled or greased with Vaseline or a similar 'release' agent. The liquid Vinamould is poured over the feature and allowed to cool to its normal flexible, rubbery consistency when it can be eased off the component you are copying. The Vinamould mould thus formed can now be filled with plaster of paris (mixed with water) and as many copies of the original made as are needed. The backs of the plaster casts are smoothed flat and can be glued into place as required.

Either dental plaster of paris, or the commercial grade, if mixed with glue size to a consistency of pouring cream takes some time to go off. When it has hardened to the consistency of putty you have about half a minute to shape it up roughly. This is very useful where you are unable to copy a piece by moulding. The plastic plaster can be roughly moulded into shape with the fingers and carved into shape as the plaster hardens off. Be sure to oil your hands before moulding the plaster though, or you will end up with as much plaster on your fingers as on the work in progress.

It is unsatisfactory to use either Brummer or other filling agents for this type of work.

Painted furniture is another problem which you may encounter. During the late Regency period particularly, ebonised furniture with brass inlays and stringing was fashionable. Sometimes gold lining or gilding was substituted for the brass. This kind of renovation is the most simple to undertake, as the black ebonising can be restored quite simply by rubbing down (or filling if deep holes are encountered) and touching in with a strong concentration of black stain. This will dry to a matt surface, and the whole piece of furniture can then be treated to one or two coats of French polish which will restore the piece to its original high gloss.

If the gold lining is seriously damaged, this should be touched in with a gold paint, made from *good quality* matching metallic powder in a clear lacquer medium. These supplies can be obtained from any art shop, or from either Windsor & Newton or Rowneys. Both make several 'shades' of gold.

At different periods 'French style' painted and gilded furniture has been in vogue and very often this painting has been applied some time after the original manufacture, often over walnut or mahogany. If this is the case you may wish to return the furniture to its original state by stripping off the paint and repolishing.

Where the groundwork of painted furniture is several coats of gesso, the chips may be quite deep and unsightly. These areas must be made good, as no amount of painting over will conceal them satisfactorily, and extensive restoration with gesso, and the subsequent rubbing down, is a long and boring business. At the same time areas where the surface is loose must be made good, as a new coat of paint will not hold loose parts in place.

Dirt and most marks can be cleaned off with white spirit, either on a soft cloth or, with care, fine wire wool. Where the paintwork has deteriorated to such an extent that repainting seems sensible, the easy way to do this is to use a suitably coloured emulsion paint. Gold decoration can be lined in with gold paint and, when dry, an 'antique' finish can be achieved by a couple of coats of ordinary French polish, fairly heavily applied with a rubber. The colour in the polish can be increased if needed by the addition of a small quantity of spirit stain.

Gold picture frames and mirror frames of good quality are usually gilded with real gold leaf and gilding is dealt with later on. Where, however, very small chips and minor damage has occurred, and the white gesso is showing through, quick and quite effective running repairs can be carried out with the use of either Treasure Gold, distributed by Windsor & Newton or Goldfinger made by Rowneys. These products are 'gold' powders, carried in a wax base, which are applied either with the tip of your finger or with a cloth. They can be burnished up quite satisfactorily with a soft brush and are produced in a range of different tones to match most gilding. A clear lacquer applied with an artist's water colour brush will further increase the reflective qualities and prevent tarnishing taking place.

Finally a few words must be said about furniture decorated by artists. This was widely practised in the middle ages and the addition of coats of arms, floral sprays or classical designs, persisted sporadically until the 18th Century. It was revived by Robert Adam who produced comprehensive interior designs for entire rooms and incorporated painted borders and medallions on satinwood and harewood furniture.

The artist, Angelica Kauffmann, had great influence on furniture decoration during this period and stimulated a host of copyists to such an extent that by the end of the Century painting rivalled marquetry as a form of furniture decoration.

Restoration of painting on furniture calls for a degree of artistic talent, particularly in the accurate mixing of colours. Here again it is most satisfactory to start with pigments in powder form and grind them in turps before mixing into a clear lacquer or goldsize medium. By doing this true colour values can be achieved and drying is reasonably rapid. If ordinary oil paints are used, the drying period is lengthy and there is a risk of smudging when applying the final finish.

Gilding
Traditionally two forms of gilding were practised, the most sophisticated being water gilding which is achieved by laying thin sheets of real gold leaf on to a polished gesso base which has been coated with parchment size. The leaf is pressed into indentations with cotton wool. After three or four hours drying time the surface may be burnished with an agate burnisher, and finally with a short bristled brush. Water gilding is an extremely expert craft and should not be undertaken without suitable tuition.

The second method is oil gilding where either four hour goldsize or Japan gold size, which dries in about 2 hours, is substituted for the parchment size. Normally oil gilding cannot be burnished.

The technique for oil gilding is as follows:

The surface to be gilded is repaired, all cracks are filled. Existing gilding is brightened up by wiping over with a clean cloth, damped with weak ammonia solution and thoroughly dried off. The surfaces to be gilded are now coated with four hour goldsize and left until the surface is nearly dry, but just tacky enough. With a four hour goldsize you have to wait about two hours for it to go tacky, and you then have a further two hours in which to work. The art is to catch the goldsize at just the right time. If it is too dry the gold leaf will not adhere; if too wet the leaf will cockle up and wrinkle.

The easiest gold leaf to use is transfer gold, each sheet of which is lightly held by wax on a piece of tissue paper. This makes handling much easier. Sheets of transfer gold are about 3 inches square and come in books of 25 sheets. The leaf is applied so that each square slightly overlaps the preceding one, each join being in the same direction. Light pressure with a cotton wool pad will transfer the leaf from the tissue to the work. Mouldings and carvings are gilded in the same way. Using an artist's brush of suitable size, press the gold into the corners and then rub carefully in the direction of the overlap to blend the sheets together and produce an even surface. This surface cannot be burnished. If you are repairing burnished work, you can achieve quite a good match by double gilding. To do this you can apply beeswax polish to the newly gilded surface as soon as it has been laid and burnish it lightly with a short bristle brush, such as a soft shoe brush. As soon as the wax is bearly dry apply a second coat of gold leaf. The second coat will adhere to the tacky wax and this can now be burnished immediately with a stiff bristle brush.

When matching up to existing work it is imperative that the base colour on the areas for repair is identical to that of the rest of the work. There is a considerable 'shine through' of the base colour and unless they match, the repaired areas will show up a different shade of gold. Both red and yellow under-coats are common in gilding and you will often notice on old gilt furniture small patches where the coloured undercoat has been exposed. Many people consider that this effect adds to the charm of an antique. In order to copy this effect, you can 'distress' the newly gilded areas by rubbing away some of the gold leaf on highlights. In cases where gilded furniture is liable to regular handling, it is advisable to lacquer the work with a clean Japan lacquer (obtainable from artists' material dealers).

Gold leaf illumination, such as motifs, lining, etc., can of course be done, painting with Japan goldsize only the areas where the design is required. In these cases the goldsize should be tinted to the suitable background colour. Details such as veins of a leaf, faces, etc., can then be painted over the gold leaf base after gilding.

Chapter 16

PROTECTING YOUR ANTIQUES FROM
CENTRAL HEATING

All antique furniture is made from wood that was originally air dried to have a moisture content of between twelve and fifteen per cent. For this to be maintained, the atmospheric relative humidity in your house should always be between fifty five and sixty five per cent. During the winter months, if you have efficient central heating, the relative humidity can easily drop to twenty per cent and this can cause untold damage to your antiques.

You therefore need an efficient humidifier to restore the correct balance of humidity and an instrument to inform you when the air is too dry. A variety of suitable devices are available and you can obtain all the help and advice you need from The Humidifier Advisory Service, 21 Napier Road, Bromley, Kent—Phone 01 460 1118.

It is not only wooden furniture which suffers from too dry an atmosphere—pictures, ivory, paper and books, textiles and, believe it or not, even some types of ceramics and glass can be adversely affected to a greater or lesser extent. Apart from all this, your health suffers. This sounds like a pretty good case for buying a humidifier to protect the contents of your home, but let us examine in greater detail what happens to antique furniture in adverse conditions, and to do this I refer to Miss Anne Moncrieff of the Conservation Department of the Victoria and Albert Museum.

Changes in relative humidity may be both seasonal and sudden, particularly in the winter time when heating is turned

123

on and off. A twenty per cent difference in relative humidity may occur during a period as short as twenty-four hours. Similar changes can occur on a twelve hour cycle if room heating is turned off at night and on again in the morning. Ideally, temperature should be controlled by a thermostat and humidification by an automatic humidistat.

When the humidity in the air goes down, it starts leeching the moisture from such things as furniture. This results in cracks and splits, appearing especially in veneered and inlaid furniture. Joints may loosen because the animal glue with which they are made dries out and crystallizes. Fluctuations in relative humidity are the most damaging of all to works of art because the materials follow the humidity changes with their own inversely proportional uptake and loss of moisture, giving rise to expansion and contraction.

It is true to say that more damage has been done to antiques by central heating in the last twenty-five years than in the two or three hundred years before its introduction. In the houses of our parents and grandparents, heating was by coal fires. These produced draughts that introduced damp air continually into the rooms and kept the moisture content of the air at an acceptable level. If the rooms became too cold and damp, moulds sometimes formed on furniture and certainly moisture condensed on polished surfaces from time to time, but this did not do any great or lasting damage to the furniture.

Too dry an atmosphere will cause cracks and movements in joints; veneers and marquetry to lift or split as it moves against the carcase wood; warping of panels, bureau and coffer lids; distorting of metal inlays; cracking and loosening of gesso, paint, varnishes and oriental lacquer work; loosening of joints in chair backs and table legs.

Wood swells and shrinks in response to moisture changes and does this more in one direction in respect of the grain of the timber than it does in the other. Movement in response to relative humidity changes is twice as great for plain as it is for quarter sawn timber and it is because of this different degree of swelling in different directions that wood has this particular tendency to distort.

An old piece of furniture constructed originally at fifteen per cent moisture content and now subjected to centrally heated conditions, with no humidification, will have its moisture content reduced to approximately eleven per cent and this will, of course, incur considerable damage. Shrinkage will occur with an alarming rate of about 0.2 in. per foot. If, as occasionally occurs, the conditions become even drier, the moisture content would be further reduced perhaps to seven per cent, resulting in a shrinkage of 0.3 in. per foot.

Tests on old wood have shown that it does not lose its tendency to move with changes of relative humidity in the air as it gets older, which means that considerable movements will take place every year from winter to summer, and in the highly variable conditions found in this country, probably several times a year. If the heating is turned off every night, movement is probably taking place twice a day!

The damage to furniture takes different forms depending on the structure of the piece. Tables made of two boards pegged together edge to edge will show shrinkage. The joints between the boards will open up perceptibly and the pegs become loose. The exposed ends of boards lose moisture before the rest, contracting more quickly causing splits which can be seen at the ends of most old wide boards. In an attempt to stop warping and keep wide boards flat, 'cleats' or 'clamps' were fastened to each end with their grain at right angles to that of the board. When such a construction dries out, relief from the resulting strain is achieved by breaks and splits appearing in a number of different places.

In more complex furniture, embellished with plain and in-laid veneers and marquetry on a ground or carcase of another timber, contraction often takes place, splitting and warping the ground and causing the tearing of the applied veneer in a way which is both unsightly and difficult to repair. In some cases, a combination of ground shrinkage and loss of adhe-sion of the glue itself leads to loosening of the veneers, and where they run across the grain of the ground they buckle due to the area of the ground becoming smaller than that of the veneer because of different amounts of shrinkage in the different types of wood.

This effect is particularly marked in Boule furniture where metal, especially brass, forms part of the marquetry and which, because it is unaffected by humidity, cannot shrink and is forced to buckle away from the ground.

When veneers are glued to one side only, across the grain of the ground wood, only the back can shrink on drying, and the panel warps. Paint, varnish and lacquer may also cause warping by preventing swelling only on one side of the panel.

It can therefore be seen that if you have any valuable antiques, or indeed if you want to protect your modern furniture, you should take steps to stabilize the humidity in your house and that this is particularly important in winter time.

Several types of humidifiers are available and can be classified under five headings.

(a) Steam evaporation (electric)
(b) Fan induced absorption operated (electric)
(c) Atomisation (electric)
(d) Instant Steam (electric)
(e) Hang on radiator humidifiers (non-electric).

It is important to avoid so called humidifiers which evaporate only a fraction of a pint of water a day. This applies to trays, bowls and jars of water and very small 'hang on' radiator humidifiers.

The type of humidifier most likely to suit an efficiently centrally heated house is one that gives what is known as *Positive Humidification*. This means adding sufficient water vapour to the dry air to raise the relative humidity to exactly the correct level to restore comfort conditions and stabilize the movement of the timber in your furniture at its correct level. This can only be achieved by an electric humidifier, which preferably has an adjustable output capable of producing at least one pint per hour. Ideally the humidifier should be wired in conjunction with a humidistat which can be set at the correct level of relative humidity for the desired temperature so that it will regulate the output of the humidifier to maintain this level.

The Humidifier Advisory Service will assist you in your choice of the correct installation.

Chapter 17

HOW TO EXAMINE ANTIQUES

In these days of mass communication, where the prices of everything from meat and bread to package holidays are nightly discussed on television, and daily 'exposed' in the press, the non-expert (which is most of us) has every right to feel baffled over the right price to pay for non-standard, non-mass produced articles. Antique furniture obviously faces you, the would-be buyer, with the problem of making up your mind how much you are prepared to pay for any given article.

But perhaps you are only interested in buying dilapidated and broken articles, suitable for you to practise restoration and renovation—furniture in such a sorry state that the dealer should be glad of the chance to get it off his hands. It therefore comes as quite a shock, particularly at auction sales, to see what, on the surface, appears to be near junk changing hands for dozens, sometimes scores or even hundreds of pounds, and apparently first-class articles failing to attract a bid of more than fifty pence or perhaps a pound.

Part of the answer is that the professional antique dealer has a trained eye and can spot a good 18th Century piece, assess its potential, visualise it after it has been renovated and restored, estimate the probable cost of restoration and arrive at a figure that he is prepared to bid. There is an insatiable demand for antique furniture and an ever increasing supply of old furniture available. The result has been a rapid increase in interest in Victorian and Edwardian furniture with a consequent meteoric rise in the prices paid for presentable examples of the furnishings of the 19th Century.

With all furniture, the determining factor governing its price is its acceptability and usefulness in a modern house. As a generalisation, Victorian homes had larger rooms and loftier ceilings than those of the mid and late 20th Century and, in consequence, very large pieces of furniture are too big to fit in to our smaller and lower rooms. It therefore follows that a small Victorian chest of drawers of poor quality and indifferent condition can command a higher price than a very large chest of 'superior' workmanship of the same period. Such articles as eight and a half foot high display cabinets or linen presses are even less saleable to the average buyer, and pieces of furniture no longer used much in the home, such as wardrobes—even when they are of first class quality—only fetch a few pounds.

How then do you set about determining how much you should pay for a piece of furniture? Judging its age, condition, degree of alteration or restoration and its true value.

To begin with, any article is worth as much as someone is prepared to pay for it, and this to some extent is determined by their reason for buying. Over the last few years a lot of people have been buying antiques because they think they are going to increase in value more rapidly and steadily than other forms of investment and, as a result, have acquired a large number of pups.

It is very dangerous to pay out good money for a thing just because someone says it is bound to go up in value. The attitude must always be that it is going to beautify your home and give enduring pleasure or be a useful possession, performing constant service. When all is said and done, you are likely to have the thing around for some time, and, if you hate it, it doesn't matter how much it is worth.

Having established the motivation for purchasing something, some research has to be done to find out what exactly you are considering buying and the true value of the article. As far as antiques are concerned, there are a number of useful guides that you can acquire. Perhaps the best is *The Price Guide to Antique Furniture*, published by the Antique

Collectors Club, Clapton, Woodbridge, Suffolk. This book overcomes the problem of rapidly changing values by publishing every six months a price revision list for which the subscription is £1.50 a year. Much more comprehensive, but lacking in descriptions of the individual items illustrated, is *The Lyle Official Antiques Review*. This book is produced annually and is based on the average of prices fetched in auction rooms during the year preceding publication. It is obtainable from Lyle Publications, 7 Liverpool Terrace, Worthing, Sussex. There are also a host of other publications designed for the specialist collector, dealing in their own particular fields.

These books give a useful indication of the rough value of any piece of furniture; they do not and, of course, cannot give any more than an indication of the quality or condition in which any particular piece is offered. It is at this stage that your own judgment has to come into play and there is no doubt that the development of this judgment offers a lifetime of pleasure and enjoyment to the collector.

Here I can give no more than an indication of how to go about examining and assessing a piece of furniture. Experience, the longer the better, is the only real way to acquire knowledge. There are many pitfalls and even experts get caught out from time to time, so you need not be ashamed of exhibiting your ignorance. Nobody can know all about everything in the antique business—that is why so many good people, dealers and collectors alike, eventually specialise in one branch of the field.

It must be appreciated that antiques pass through a number of hands in the trade before they are finally bought by someone who is actually going to use them. Every dealer is going to make a profit—or else he will not be in business for very long—and the nearer you buy to Bond Street or Kensington, the higher the price is likely to be, although there is a bargain in every dealer's shop if you are clever enough to spot it.

Of course there is always the compensation that the more reputable the dealer is, the greater his degree of integrity and the larger the amount of information he will volunteer about the piece you are examining. When buying from a top flight dealer, you are purchasing not only an antique but part of his knowledge, his guarantee of authenticity; his very valuable opinion and any first class restoration that was required to put the article into perfect condition. You are also paying a proportion of his overheads which are very much higher than the back street junk man or the market trader.

The greatest bargains undoubtedly come from house clearances, and there are thousands of dealers who specialise in this. This is most likely the source of most of the antiques that come back on the market, and often the people who do it have no more than an inkling of top values. They usually are interested only in a quick turnover and, by necessity, collect far more junk than good merchandise. Their prices too are often lower than those of the auction rooms.

In the auction rooms you are up against the rest of the world, including a fair number of dealers who have the advantage of knowing every trick and may not be averse to 'bidding a piece up' to discourage the casual purchaser. You, however, providing you are sure of your ground and have decided on the absolute maximum price you are prepared to pay can bid with conviction, have the edge over the dealer because you are going to keep the piece while he has to sell it again at a profit. He has to pay for any restoration work where you are going to do it yourself. He has considerable overheads while you have none. But make sure you are not bidding against another enthusiastic amateur and get carried away by the excitement of the battle. There is a lot of technique to buying at auction deserving of close observation and considerable study.

You must work at becoming an expert in your chosen field, and the sources of knowledge are museums and books. Read up on the subject, attend lectures at museums, join a club like the National Association of Decorative and Fine Arts, or The Antique Collectors Club; talk to the specialists at Antique Fairs and collections open to the public; above all acquire a sense of period and style.

It is important to get the feel of antiques. This you cannot do fully in museums and collections, for here you are not allowed to handle the things displayed. You can however do this at Antique Fairs and in shops and auction rooms during the viewing time. Learn to be very, very patient and look slowly, only buying after you have examined minutely the object of immediate interest. If the style is right, if the condition is right, if you can make good use of it and it will fit into your home, if you like it and think it is more or less correctly priced, buy it on the spot. If you wait until tomorrow, someone else will have taken advantage of your hesitation.

So how do you set about examining a piece of furniture! First of all, if it is between one and four hundred years old, it will bear a number of honourable battle scars. Several generations of servants and children will have left their marks. Half the charm of antiques is that they are old—if they do not look old, if they are just too perfect, be suspicious, either they have been recently restored, or they are not what they seem to be. A lot of reproduction furniture was produced in late Victorian and Edwardian times, and during the nineteen twenties. Much of it was good and may now look superficially authentic. I am not decrying these early reproductions; many of them are excellent and can be bargains, but they are nevertheless reproductions and not worth as much as true period pieces. Beware, particularly, of 'Chippendale, Sheraton and Hepplewhite' chairs: there never have been enough sets of good chairs.

Look for true patination, or the remnants of patina, on the interiors of drawers, the undersides. Often a piece of 18th Century furniture was repolished by our Victorian antecedents, who loved highly polished, what we would today consider over polished, furniture. Sometimes only the tops have been polished leaving the original patina on the front and sides.

Look in the cracks and mouldings for evidence of accumulated dust, ground into the polish, giving a variation of tone and colour. Look for light patches where the original stain and polish has been worn away by constant dusting. Look for dark patches where there should have been constant handling. Pay close attention to feet and legs, this is where maximum wear and tear takes place, both through knocking with brooms and cleaners and because old stone floors were often damp and the feet were originally fixed on to furniture to raise them above the damp level. If the feet are perfect they most likely have been replaced, and the dealer should tell you that they have.

Many pieces of antique furniture are what are known as marriages. Like the apple pie in the canteen, the crust and the fruit only met on the plate! Tables are fitted with new tops. Bed posts are turned into torcheres by adding a base and flat top. A tallboy can be turned into two chests of drawers by adding a new top. Double height corner cupboards can be made from two separate hanging cupboards. Wardrobes can be converted into break front bookcases, linen chests can be made into secretaire bookcases. Cheval mirror supports are used to make up sofa tables. The list is seemingly endless.

Beware of the out-of-the-ordinary piece of furniture. There were very few 18th Century eccentrics who had specially designed furniture made to suit their own tastes. Most pieces can be traced back to the pattern books of well known designers and any 'unusual' or very rare pieces stand a very good chance of having been 'made up' from bits.

Always examine the backs and underneath of a piece of furniture. It is here that you will discover if a piece has been recently altered or renovated. After you have examined a few pieces you will soon be able to detect if they have been tampered with. Even the under sides of pieces of furniture acquire the patina of age which cannot be imitated with stain or artificial dirt. Anyrate, no reputable professional restorer will attempt to deceive. At most he will stain over the concealed parts of newly cut wood and newly positioned glue blocks, and this is obvious to the most inexperienced eye, once alerted to spot the signs of recent repairs. The edges of the back timber should be stained and there should be no new raw joints. There should be no joints in the length of the boards and often the timber will have been painted with faded red lead primer. Joints between boards may have been sealed with strips of linen, glued on with animal glue.

This is also a good time to look at nails and screws (if any are visible). Old nails were cut by hand and are quite distinctive when compared with modern ones. In the area surrounding 18th Century nails you will always see telltale dark stains, caused by two hundred years of rusting and oxidisation; new nails will always be bright, even when they have been stained over, the brightness will show up if they are scratched with a penknife.

Next examine the drawers. Early oak furniture, before the late 17th Century rarely had drawer runners, the drawers running on the drawer bottoms. The best quality English furniture was oak lined, and the drawers were also constructed of *thin* oak boards. Up to about 1770 the grain of the bottom boards of drawers ran from front to back, thereafter from side to side. Often with grooved supporting stay in the centre of long drawers to counteract bowing and shrinkage. In many pieces the drawer runners will have been worn away by constant use, the maximum wear being towards the back of the drawer. No 18th Century drawer would have reached to the back of the carcase, but would have been 'stopped' by small wooden blocks on the bottom rail separating the drawers. No drawer before 1800 would have mouldings fitted to the interior joints. If the wear on drawer runners was so deep that the drawer fronts tilt back out of perpendicular, new runners may have been fitted beside the original runners at a later date. The quality of this work will give an indication of the quality of the restoration. If pins or nails have been used, the piece will have been 'tarted up' to sell, as subsequent wear will expose the steel panel pins and they will tear into the carcase in time.

The drawer sides should have been dovetailed into the fronts. English cabinet makers in the 18th Century made very small dovetails, well spaced. Continental cabinet makers' dovetails are much larger and inclined to look clumsy. Old drawers have a scribe mark where the dovetail ends, modern dovetails are made with a dovetailing jig and are close together, absolutely evenly spaced, and there is no scribe mark as they are machine cut.

Now the handles should be examined. With old pieces, you may find evidence of several different kinds of handles being fitted at different times. Brass pear drop, or acorn drop handles were fitted to the late 17th and early 18th Century walnut furniture and cast brass plate handles were also fitted a little later. In Victorian times these were often removed and replaced by turned wooden handles at the dictate of current fashion. Recently these wooden handles have been removed and again replaced with reproduction brass handles. If the back plates seem rather too large, they may be concealing the ravages caused by handle replacement. Early brass handles were all brass, even the nuts. The threads were hand cut and, in consequence, rather coarse and look hand made. Most reproduction handles have steel threaded shafts screwed into brass pommels and are secured with square or hexagonal steel nuts. They are very easy to identify. All old brasswork is a different colour from modern brass as it contains more copper and, in consequence, has a subtly distinctive look to it.

Key escutcheons sometimes give a clue to age. 18th Century escutcheons always had a rounded bottom, unlike later ones which have a square bottom, but reproduction 18th Century escutcheons are still made so look at the colour.

If a piece of furniture has cross banding or fine line inlay, known as stringing, this can give a good idea of age. Much early walnut furniture had a herringbone inlay running in a clockwise direction around the edges of drawers and tops. If you run your fingers over the surface of early herringbone inlays, you will be able to feel unevenness where shrinkage over the years has forced it up a bit in places. If it is absolutely flat, the chances are that it has been relaid or even replaced in parts.

Stringing can also be an indication of age; they are usually made of boxwood and ebony. A single white or black string running round the edge, or a combination of fairly broad black and white strings was normal during the 18th Century. If, however, the stringing is fine and contains an intricate pattern, the stringing is Victorian or Edwardian.

On 18th Century chests of drawers and bureaux, the drawers should be graduated from top to bottom and bureaux, particularly, should have four drawers on the front varying in depth from about four inches to six inches. Better chests of drawers were often fitted with a brushing slide just above the top drawer. This enhances the value of the piece.

Much Sheraton and Hepplewhite furniture has square, tapered legs. The tapering must always be on the insides of the legs and the leg should run straight through from the floor to the top of the piece. Look with suspicion at any piece that has a moulding running across the leg where the carcase begins. It may have been applied to cover the join where new legs have been put on at a later date. Late Sheraton furniture sometimes had 'bandages' of veneer added as decoration to the lower leg. Here, again, these can have been added at a later date after the legs had been extended, or where a leg had broken off, to cover the repair joint. Heavy sideboards are particularly susceptible to leg breakage, so examine them carefully, particularly if there are applied bandages on the legs.

Turned legs on any piece of furniture are desirable, particularly if they are also reeded or fluted. The thinner and spindlier the legs are, the earlier and the better. This is particularly true of Pembroke and other drop-leaf tables. The Victorians liked their furniture solid, and it shows. The legs on tables are important too, dining tables of the 18th Century were, more often than not, constructed on two or more sets of tripod legs. The weakest part of these tripods is where the leg is dovetailed into the central pillar. Examine these carefully to see if they are sprung or in any way cracked or shattered. They should not be held in with screws or strengthened underneath with iron brackets. Screw holes are often concealed with stopper or a wooden plug, so look for these. If a leg is sprung, another trick is to level them up by inserting wedges under the feet.

Always look at the proportions of any piece of furniture. If the proportions of an 18th Century piece look wrong, it most likely is wrong and has been cut down or otherwise altered. Thomas Sheraton particularly, in *The Cabinet-Maker and Upholsterers Drawing-Book*, published between 1791 and 1802, went to great lengths to demonstrate the importance of proportion and perspective. The Adams, too, who were primarily architects, placed great emphasis on the importance of balance and correct proportion.

Upholstery, and the evidence of re-upholstery, is also an indication of age. It is reasonable to assume that chair coverings will require renewing every thirty years or so, say three times a Century. The seat rails of chairs therefore indicate by the number of tack holes how many times they have been re-upholstered. Sometimes the rails become so butchered that they have to be replaced. Normally chair bottoms are covered by tacking on a dust cover. In good antique shops these will be left loose, so that you are able to examine the rails.

With veneered furniture, you should if possible observe the thickness of the veneers. Old veneers were all cut by hand and in consequence all vary slightly in thickness. Some are up to 3/16th" thick. Good quality veneers are close grained and often beautifully marked. Eighteenth Century cabinet makers kept the best of their veneers for door panels and the tops of cabinets. The quality of the figuring obviously affects the value of any piece.

Later on veneers were machine cut, sometimes paper thin in late Victorian times. Today veneers are sold as either single or double knife cut, the latter being half the thickness of the former. Sawn veneers are virtually unobtainable except by soaking them off old discarded pieces of furniture. Good restorers saw cut their own veneers, but only for the repair of relatively small areas. If part of the grain on a piece of furniture appears to be somewhat rough or more open grained than the rest, the chances are that the areas has been repaired.

In conclusion, the more pieces of furniture you examine and handle, the more information you will acquire and the more knowledgeable you will become. Undoubtedly some of the best judges of antique furniture are auctioneers' cataloguers and porters—they handle more furniture than any one else and they observe the prices they fetch under the hammer. Your approach to any dealer is important if you want to secure his co-operation. All good dealers are willing and anxious to tell you as much as they can about anything in which you express interest. Very few dealers are trying to catch you out, but they have every reason to feel annoyed if you insist on pointing out to them every minor imperfection that you can find in the article under examination.

If you suspect that any article has been recently restored, ask—you are entitled to know. If you suspect it may be a Victorian reproduction of an 18th Century style, again seek the opinion of the person selling it. If you receive evasive answers, then you can assume the worst and look elsewhere. Remember that antiques, like all other goods, are covered by the Description of Goods Act and if you are misled deliberately you can claim your money back.

In fact, you will find that many dealers, when selling any major item, will offer to take the article back at cost if you are not satisfied with it after you have tried it in your home. They may even extend this promise for as much as twelve months.

You are always going to find wide fluctuations in price for similar pieces of antique furniture. There are far too many reasons to explain this phenomena in detail. It is always up to you to find the bargains, and know one when you see it. Demand for certain items, and the price that they will fetch, fluctuates from district to district. Most 'runners'—that is traders who buy from one dealer and sell to another—stay in business and make a reasonable living because they know this. They know where they can buy Windsor chairs in Warwickshire and sell them at a profit in Cambridge; buy tripod tables in Cambridge and sell them in Essex; buy brass beds in Essex and sell them in Warwickshire. Some runners sell the entire stock from their van three times in a single day—but not every day.

Remember, too, that a dealer likes to deal. Never hesitate to ask him if he will reduce his price—he may be over-stocked or in need of ready cash and be prepared to take a reduction for an immediate sale.

And finally, and possibly of greatest importance of all, remember that just because a piece of furniture has been restored, or has been altered, or is in some way imperfect, it does not have to be despised or rejected. The only difference between it and a perfect undamaged article is that it is worth less money. It is up to you to decide if it is worth the asking price to you. The very best, top drawer pieces of furniture come with complete authentication, very occasionally with the original bill of sale or with the makers mark on it. Alas, this is the rare exception.

Any good dealer will give you a bill of sale with as full a description and authentication as he can. You are entitled to this, so be sure you get it. And keep it carefully—in a hundred years' time it will be worth a lot, both in interest and in value to your grandchildren, for antiques are going to be in demand for a long time to come.

And oh yes—good hunting!

Chapter 18

RECOGNISING STYLE AND PERIOD

The earliest English furniture which survives in any quantity dates from the reign of the Tudors and is constructed of oak. Undoubtedly other woods, such as elm, beech, ash and fruitwoods were also used but, being less durable, most has long ago disintegrated. Construction at first was of a very simple nature and the articles in use were utilitarian. Both design and decoration was greatly influenced by the Gothic Architecture of the Church.

The chest or coffer was possibly the first and most common article of furniture which, while serving as a receptacle for valuables, also doubled as a table and a seat. They, like all subsequent furniture, were constructed of five planks (plus lid), joined together with willow pegs.

Next in importance was the bed, which was a simple frame of four rails, bored with regular spaced holes through which ropes were stretched to form a woven net making a base to support a mattress.

Five board stools were used as seats and were placed near to the walls which were used to lean against. Tables were of simple plank construction, supported on trestles.

1500–1600

With the introduction of the mortice and tenon joint method of construction in the 15th Century, the craft of joiner or joyner was introduced and more elaborate seats, known as joint or joyned stools, came into use. At the same time it was

TUDOR PERIOD 1500–1603
Four poster bed 1590. Five board stool. Ambury or food cupboard. Joint stool. Coffer.

found that thin panels of wood, held loosely in joined frames, were more durable as this method of construction allowed sufficient natural expansion and contraction to take place to prevent cracking of the panels. This form of manufacture was standard practice into the 17th Century.

In the mid 16th Century the Renaissance influence was introduced by Flemish and other low countries craftsmen and heavily turned and carved legs on tables, cupboards and buffets became the fashion. The puff sleeves and pantaloons of Henry VIII and Elizabeth I are reflected in the decorated posts of their four poster beds and other furniture. The affluence of the reign of the first Elizabeth was undoubtedly partly responsible for the development of many new pieces of furniture, like the court (Norman French for short) cupboard, used to display 'flaggons, cans, cups and beakers'. Cupboards fitted with pierced doors known as aumbries, used for food storage. Linen and clothes cupboards, known as presses and the earliest of corner cupboards.

1625–1649

Charles I, who married Henrietta of France, had profound influence on the design of English furniture. He was a scholar and a patron of the arts and opened up far Eastern trade through his support of the East India Company. Hence began the vogue for Japan Lacquer work cabinets and the use of French and Spanish walnut to build much lighter and more elegant furniture. Chairs, upholstered in fine imported silks, velvets and Spanish leathers came into use outside the bedroom. They were wide and solid, with low backs and arms to allow the gentlemen, wearing their swords, to sit sideways and sprawl.

1649–1688

During Oliver Cromwell's short Puritan revolution furniture was plain and austere. The gateleg table with the barley sugar twist leg became popular, but it was with the restoration that real extravagance in furniture design was given full rein. Charles II; his Court; his Spanish wife, and his Dutch mistress, brought back to England their tastes for continental

STUART & CAROLEAN *1603–1675*
Elbow chair, 1620. Walnut arm chair, 1665. Long case lacquered clock. Restoration
Day bed, 1660. Barley sugar leg table, 1660.

elegance and a passion for collecting 'curiosities'. During this age was born the first generation of antique dealers, who sold porcelain lacquer and glass, clocks, old coins, medals, cameos, and the new-fangled barometers. Far Eastern jade and carvings. On 20th May 1690 one John Hervey, first Earl of Bristol "Paid for dear wife at curiosity shop ten shillings". The well known London dealers were Medina the Jew, John van Collema and Elizabeth Genva.

The backs of chairs grew long and the carving on furniture became more intricate. George Villiers, Duke of Buckingham, started making plate glass mirrors in Vauxhall and these were contained in carved and often gilded frames. Split cane seating was introduced and the boudoir or bedroom became the venue for smart entertaining, bringing with it beautiful dressing tables, day beds and the earliest writing bureaux.

The folding gateleg table with barley sugar legs remained in popularity and, of course, it was the era of the first long case clocks and Samuel Pepys designed his famous book cases with glass doors.

1689–1714

Queen Mary II, daughter of James II, and her husband, William III, came from Holland to rule England jointly, and were succeeded in 1702 by Anne, the daughter of James II, sister of Mary. This was the great age of walnut furniture and the development of distinctive design, influenced by the culture of the low countries.

The chest of drawers, very often supported on bulbous turned legs or bun feet, replaced the coffer or cupboard as a storage unit. Both chair backs and wigs became taller. Oyster wood (laburnum), Burr Walnut, Burr Elm and Mulberry veneers of great beauty were applied to Oak carcases. X-shape stretchers were fitted to tables and stands. Sumptuous wing chairs were popular, broad in the beam to accommodate the ladies' voluminous skirts, luxuriously upholstered with tapestries, velvets and silk brocades. Many had elaborately scrolled arms.

Seaweed Marquetry, surpassing the craftsmanship of

WALNUT PERIOD 1689–1725
William & Mary bureau, 1690. Marquetry chest on stand, 1680. Elbow chair, 1690.
Wing armchair, 1730. Queen Anne elbow chair, 1720. Bureau bookcase, 1710.

the Dutch furniture makers, was produced in England. Marquetry was gradually superceded by attractively figured surfaces contained in cross banding and herringbone stringing and borders. The back of dining chairs was lowered and acquired an elegant curve to fit the back and accommodate the skirted coats of the gentlemen. The Queen Anne chair acquired the cabriole leg, most likely an importation from China and the back legs became curved and splayed to counteract the tendency of the user to rock back: a superb piece of ergonomic design, made by dedicated craftsmen. The pad foot was also introduced and, shortly after, the ball and claw foot, beautifully carved.

The chest on stand was a forerunner to the tallboy and the beautiful kneehole dressing tables, side tables and writing tables, all beautifully small and perfectly proportioned, became favourite pieces of furniture. Bureaux and Bureaux Bookcases, some of them only two foot six inches wide, and jewels of tiny kneehole desks, were also produced to furnish the comfortable intimate rooms used for everyday living. All were fitted with charmingly designed brass handles of either pear drop or pierced back plate design.

1714–1760

The reigns of the first three Georges, spanning roughly the first three quarters of the 18th Century, were the golden age of English furniture. It saw the first introduction of mahogany about 1720, most likely by the great cabinet makers of London who lived and worked in St. Pauls Churchyard, Soho and Shoreditch. This introduction was gradual and by the end of George I's reign mahogany was the fashionable furniture wood.

Influenced by William Kent, the Palladian style became popular. Chairs became lower and lighter in construction. Between 1740 and 1800 the best known craftsmen and designers of furniture were all in business. Chippendale, Sheraton, Hepplewhite and the Adam Brothers produced and published books of Designs. Thomas Chippendale's *The Gentleman's and Cabinet Makers Directory* in 1754. Thomas

Sheraton produced *The Cabinet-Maker and Upholsterers Drawing Book* in 1791, and Hepplewhite's widow published his *Cabinet Maker and Upholsterers Guide* in 1788. All these designs were widely copied and adapted by cabinet makers all over the country.

Chippendale produced three distinct design styles: Rococo, Gothic and Chinese. The scrolls, acanthus foliage and ribbon carving of the Rococo style Chippendale chairs are very distinctive. The Gothic revival, led by Horace Walpole from his house in Strawberry Hill, has left its mark on the design of the period, and the vogue for Chinese Design was perpetuated by other designers as well as the Chippendales. Of particular note is the work of Lightfoot whose Chinese Room at Clayton House, Bucks, is a unique example.

Thomas Sheraton, born in Stockton-on-Tees in 1751, was a great proponent of perspective and proportion, though his perspective drawings, most often without scale, are of doubtful value. However he published a large number of illustrations of designs of great delicacy, favouring the square back chair and long, tapered square or fluted legs, and bottom rails. He designed light and very feminine tea tables, indeed all of his designs were light and look far more frail than in fact they are.

Hepplewhite favoured oval and shield back chair designs, often incorporating an urn, or Prince of Wales feathers designs, and draped swashes in the splats. He liked delicately tapered, splayed or decorated legs with spade feet on his furniture, and produced many elaborately inlaid, and later painted designs. Hepplewhite chests of drawers are very plain with splayed feet. Many are bow fronted and sometimes have a carved apron. Handles favoured by Hepplewhite were oval or round. His sideboards were extremely delicate, usually bow fronted with a single shallow drawer in the centre; cupboards either side sometimes with a shallow drawer below. They have square tapered legs with spade feet.

Card and Gaming tables were produced in great variety of design; mostly with folding tops and a swing-out back leg to support the open table. Chests of drawers of this period are much sought after. Most popular today are the serpentine

EARLY 18TH CENTURY 1720–1750
Mid-century tallboy. Bureau/Cupboard. Early Chippendale kneehole desk. George II gaming table. Strawberry Hill gothic chair. Early Chippendale cabriole leg dining chair. Sideboard, 1785.

LATE 18TH CENTURY 1750–1800
*Hepplewhite dining chair. Late 18th century occasional table. Sheraton ladies' writing
desk. Adam style commode. Chinese Chippendale chairs. Late 18th century bedroom
commode with tombour door.*

front designs or the square front varieties with bracket or splayed feet.

During this period too, tea drinking became a popular and polite method of afternoon entertainment in the home. This led to the production of special furniture for the taking of tea. Many circular tea tables, supported by a centre pillar tripod of three cabriole legs, were manufactured. The best of them had 'piecrust' edges and either carved ball and claw, or pad feet. Teapot stands, butlers trays, oval and kidney shaped tea trays also made their first appearance.

1760–1800

By 1760 Robert Adam, having spent much time in his early years in Italy, where he absorbed the forms of classical culture, began to have an impact on the design of English furniture. Adam was basically an architect, but his neo-classical designs involved interior decoration to harmonize with his structural works. The popularisation of the sideboard is credited to him by many furniture historians, as are the knife case and the wine cooler in the form of urns, and the cellarette in the form of sarcophagus.

1800–1840

Although the actual Regency of the Prince of Wales during George III's illness only lasted nine years, the Regency Period, when applied to English furniture, covers the time from roughly the start of the French Wars into the early years of the reign of Victoria. It was a natural development from the classical revival of the time of the Adams, stimulated by a book by Thomas Hope published in 1807 *Household Furniture and Interior Decoration*. Hope had travelled extensively in Egypt, Greece, and the Middle East collecting antiques and had commissioned the making of copies of ancient classical furniture for his home. His book was quickly followed in 1808 by a book of simplified classical furniture designs by George Smith, called *A Collection of Designs for Household Furniture and Decoration*. Remember, too, that this was the period of Nelson's victories in the Middle East (Battle of Nile occupation of Greek islands, etc.) and the French Directoire

REGENCY 1810–1840
Armchair in Egyptian style. Drum library table. Reading chair. Sofa table with lyre
supports. Sideboard (circa 1805).

Style also Greek-Roman influenced which developed into French Empire.

Sphinxes, Serpents, Lyres, Lions, Egyptian Heads, Lotus Flower and Anthemion motifs cast in brass and gilded by the Ormalu process were used in profusion, mixed often with martial themes of spears, swords, drums and other military and naval paraphenalia. Brass inlays of all kinds were popular, both as plain stringing and intricate floral designs.

Chairs with low backs and sabre legs, both at the front and the back, and rails moulded in the form of a rope, appeared. Much furniture was constructed of ebony or was 'ebonized'. Dining-room tables with reeded edges, supported by similarly reeded tripod legs terminating in brass lion head castors are typical of the period, as are sofa tables and needlework tables supported on lyre shaped supports. Drum tables of all sizes were fashionable. Easy chairs and sofas were often square in construction and woven split cane was sometimes incorporated as support for leather or tapestry cushions. Nests of occasional tables on long spindly legs also appeared for the first time. New exotic woods like Zebra wood, birds eye maple, rosewood, amboyna, tulip wood were used in much greater quantity than ever before.

Parallel with this and due to some extent to the Prince Regent's interest in 'Chinoiseries' which influenced the design of the Brighton Pavilion, and earlier the Chinese Drawing-Room at Carlton House, Chinese taste was once again revived. Sheraton, Henry Holland and the Chippendale Workshops all contributed to the vogue.

1840–1900

Queen Victoria ascended the throne in 1837 and reigned for over sixty years. During the early part of her reign the widespread use of machinery had great impact on English furniture and the 1851 Exhibition set a stamp of Gothic Revival in style that can best be described as a cross between Albert Memorial and Early Bloody. The Victorians were, however, great experimenters and in spite of the atrocious design of some of the mid-reign furniture produced much that was, and still is, pleasant and acceptable by modern stan-

VICTORIAN 1840—1900
Whatnot. Ladies chair. Davenport. Spoon back chair. Wellington chest. Needlework
table. Beadwork footstool. Chaise longue. Typical Edwardian inlay.

dards. Balloon Back chairs can be pleasantly proportioned and functional. Wellington Chests and Davenports are now in great demand as are military chests and papier mache trays and tables, inlaid with mother of pearl.

There was great emphasis on comfort and deep buttoned spoon back chairs, chaise-longues, and club sofas are now in considerable demand. Indeed, even the corner whatnot, plant stands and torcheres are snapped up for renovation and use.

Late in the reign, the movement back to handcrafts led by William Morris helped to develop a new style of considerable distinction which is again being recognised as also is the later Art Nouveau cult.

Chapter 19

MISCELLANEOUS INTELLIGENCE

Bamboo

Nearly all bamboo furniture is Victorian; earlier pieces are often simulated to give the impression of being bamboo by the use of paint.

Bamboo usually shatters when it breaks, leaving a host of long splinters hanging on to the ends. As bamboo is made up of hollow segments, it can be repaired and strengthened by the insertion of suitably sized dowels into the central cavity. If a joint in the bamboo occurs (where there is no clear cavity running through the centre), this can safely be drilled out to accommodate the dowel.

The shattered ends are best repaired with epoxy resin glues, which fill in the cavities where parts of the original bamboo are missing. The resin can be suitably coloured to match the base colour with powder colours and touching in can be done when the resin has dried with oil paints. As an alternative a filler, such as plastic padding can be used and painted to match when the repair is dry.

To brighten up bamboo furniture first clean off with strong detergent and water to remove accumulated dirt and wax and then brush coat with a clear polyurethane varnish such as Furniglas PU15.

Bone and Ivory Cleaning

Both bone and ivory inlays tend to colour with age; ivory particularly if it is kept in the dark. A stiff paste made from white pumice, methylated spirits and hydrogen peroxide used as a dual scouring and bleaching powder is effective, but great care has to be taken as ivory and bone will absorb liquids and expand if wetted for too long a period.

Ivory and bone can be cleaned with safety by polishing over with methylated spirits. If persistent dirt and stains are difficult to remove, try ordinary metal polish or meths and a mild abrasive such as jeweller's rouge, fine pumice or rottenstone.

Ivory and bone are fairly easy to saw, carve or turn, but as an alternative, when parts of inlay are missing, fill the cavities with white waterproof Brummer stopper. Sandpaper down when dry; scratch in any necessary detail with a suitable tool and coat with clear polyurethane varnish or clear French polish.

Brass Cleaning and Colouring

Opinions are divided over the treatment of brass fittings. Some people like them bright, some prefer them dull. My personal preference is for something between the two, with the highlights glowing and unhandled parts slightly tarnished.

In order to clean up old brass buffing with a revolving linen mop dressed with a suitable buffing soap is by far the quickest method. An alternative is to use Horolene, a solvent cleaner used by clock repairers.

Once brass has been brought to the required degree of colour, it should not be lacquered as the lacquer deteriorates over a period of time and is difficult to remove again. Thorough waxing with ordinary wax polish keeps brass clean while allowing it to mellow. Brass should be wax polished with the rest of the furniture.

Medium wire wool impregnated with metal polish will also clean up brass effectively.

To colour brass, immerse it in a solution of Butyr of Antimony for a few minutes. This turns it black and the highlights can be brought up again by buffing. For a nut brown colour, boil in the following solution:

1 cup water
1 tablespoon Trisodium phosphate
$\frac{1}{2}$ teaspoon Liver of Sulphur

Buffing soaps and other metal finishing supplies are available from:

T. A. Hutchinson Ltd.
16 St. Johns Lane
London E.C.1.

Horolene is stocked by:
Keith Harding Ltd.
93 Hornsey Road
London N.7.

Brass fittings

Sometimes brass parts cannot be matched up from the vast stocks of merchants such as Beardmores of Percy Street, London W.1, and it is necessary to make them. Fortunately brass is an easy metal to work and parts can usually be made out of solid or sheet brass by filing and polishing or cutting out of flat brass with either a fretsaw or a bandsaw. Finishing and smoothing is best achieved with emery cloth torn into strips about $\frac{3}{4}''$ to $1''$ wide and used in the same way as a shoe shiner. Brass is also quite easy to turn if you have a lathe.

Brass inlays can be cut from sheet brass, using a paper pattern in the same way as veneer inlays described earlier. They can be held in place with epoxy resin glues without fear of coming away. It is best, however, to make a key on the side to be glued with a rasp.

A large variety of ready made brass inlays can be obtained, already inlaid into veneers from:

Intalays Ltd.
Holton Heath,
Poole, Dorset.

Canework

Cane for chair seats and backs is made from a palm called rattan and is obtainable in several sizes. Unfortunately very few chair caners are left and you may have to tackle this task yourself. If you do, you can obtain full instructions from a number of publications.

There is a chapter on this subject in The Complete Book of Furniture Repair by Ralph P. Kinney.

Fretwork

Recently broken fretwork can be joined together fairly easily by laying out on a flat board covered with two or three layers of newspaper. The elements can then be glued together and held in place while drying, with panel pins driven into the board, but not through the fretwork. Any missing pieces can be fabricated from suitable wood and glued into place. Joins of new to old wood should be bevelled to give maximum glueing area. Any surplus glue will only stick to the newspaper and can be sponged off when the completed fretwork is dry and hard.

With blind frets, or where the back does not show, the work may be further strengthened by backing with linen, in which case a layer of linen is placed between the wood and the newspaper.

Thin fretwork can easily be cut out by using a paper pattern glued to the wood to be fretted. If you have an old treadle fretsaw the work is quick. Such a machine can also be used for marquetry cutting.

Glass Cutting

As an aid to glass cutting, dip the cutting wheel into real turpentine before each cut. If you are lucky enough to have a diamond cutter a cleaner scratch can be made and less failures will be experienced.

When cutting irregular shapes, make a cardboard pattern first and fit it into the space the glass is to occupy, leaving as much free space as you can afford. Lay the pattern under the glass as a guide when cutting. Excess glass can be nibbled away with a pair of flat-nosed pliers or sharp pincers if the piece is a little too large to fit its frame.

Lay the glass on an old blanket on a flat bench or table when cutting and use a straight edge wherever possible. For curved cuts, first cut away as much surplus as possible in straight cuts and then score along the curved line, using a pattern or template. Snap off the last pieces with a pair of pliers.

INLAYS AND MARQUETRY

These have traditionally been cut by making a multiple sandwich of various kinds and colours of veneers of similar thickness, separated by layers of thick unsized paper—the kind that used to be used for sugar bags. The sandwich is glued together with thin glue and pressed between boards to ensure that it dries flat. The marquetry pattern is then cut through the whole sandwich and the different layers can easily be separated by splitting the paper used for separating each type of veneer. By interchanging the various kinds of wood, a jigsaw that fits perfectly together can be made up. You get as many inlays as you had layers of wood.

Light woods are coloured by pushing them into a bed of hot sand. Use a pair of pliers and thrust the part that you want to be darkest, edge on, into the hot sand. You will find that the deeper into the sand, the darker the colour, and that the colour will shade off evenly towards the uncovered area.

Leather and Baize Desk and Table Tops

Replacing the tops of desks, bureaux and card tables need provide no headaches if you follow these instructions. Leathers are furnished, complete with gold borders and tooling, by a number of trade suppliers. They invariably have a few inches surplus on all edges.

First check the size and central position and then, with a steel straight edge cut the selvage from two adjoining sides, ensuring that these two sides exactly fit the position they are to fill. Lay the leather aside and coat the whole area of the table to be covered with adhesive, using a serrated scraper such as is supplied with impact adhesives. This leaves little lines of the adhesive on the surface, evenly spread.

The surface must of course be quite clean and free from old glue. Any holes or cracks must be filled with Brummer filler or plastic wood and sanded down to dead flat.

The best adhesive is either flour or rice paste, or one of the new wallpaper pastes. To make flour paste, put four tablespoons of flour and a pinch of alum into a jam jar. Add enough cold water to form a fairly stiff mixture, free from any lumps. Now add boiling water slowly, stirring all the while until the mixture is of the consistency of thick cream. The pot should now be about two-thirds full and should turn from white to translucent. If it is not translucent, put it in a saucepan of hot water and boil until the colour fades. The paste may now be thinned down to a thin cream consistency with cold water.

As soon as the surface has been coated with paste, lay the corner of the leather that you have cut to shape and carefully lay the rest in place, gently pressing out any air bubbles with a soft cloth. Make sure that the cut sides fit exactly into their recess. When the whole leather is laid, roll in the edges with a paper-hanger's roller. Now trim off the salvage on the other two sides with a sharp-pointed knife. You will find that it is quite easy to follow the edges of the recess as the roller has made an indentation and the knife edge will 'feel' the sill of the recess.

The technique for laying baize or cloth is exactly the same except that you do not have to trim off two leading edges before commencing laying as there is no pattern to position.

Leather Reviving
When you have to treat leather upholstery that has started to perish, first try to revive and clean it with saddle soap—several varieties are available from leather shops. Apply saddle soap liberally with a small damp sponge, a new application every day until the leather has become pliable and silky to the touch.

An additional treatment is to rub a mixture of two parts methylated spirit and three parts castor oil into the leather, followed a day or so later by an application of castor oil alone.

The British Museum recipe for leather dressing is excellent for preserving leather and can be used regularly. The mixture is inflammable and has to be left in a ventilated place for two or three days before final buffing with a soft cloth.

| 7 oz. Lanolin | 1 fl. oz. cedarwood oil |
| $\frac{1}{2}$ oz. beeswax | 11 fl. oz. hexane |

Keep away from any kind of flame. Dissolve the beeswax in the hexane, add the lanolin and lastly the cedar oil.

Locks

In almost every case, keys for bureaux, chests, desks and cupboards have been lost. Most locks on old furniture are also in poor condition, but not usually out of order. Anyone can learn to cut simple keys in a few minutes, and nearly all locks on furniture are simple one or two lever actions. Key blanks can be purchased for a few pence each from good ironmongers, and every large town has a locksmith. Cleaning and oiling locks is simplicity itself, so don't be frightened to explore your talents as a locksmith. If you find it is too much for you, you can always take the lock to the local man and he will supply you with a key and do repairs if required.

When locks are missing it is always difficult to find a replacement which will fit. The biggest problem is to get the key hole in the lock to align with the key hole and escutcheon in the door. A secondary problem is to find a lock wih the correct size backplate to fit the previously cut recess. The answer to both these problems is to make a new backplate from a piece of sheet brass and solder or glue (with modern adhesives now used in industry—available from Alex Tiranti, 70 High St., Theale) a smaller lock in the correct position. This is done by putting the key in the lock through the escutcheon on the door. A slot has to be precut in the new back plate to allow the tongue of the lock to project. In most cases the tongue will be long enough, but in some cases you may have to solder or braze an extension on to the tongue.

Marble

Marble-topped furniture is once again becoming popular and instead of replacing a marble top with a wooden one, you may want to recondition and polish the marble.

For light cleaning use kitchen soap and ammonia water (10% household ammonia in warm water). If the piece has been standing outside, or in a damp place, fungus growth may be present, in which case use a fungicide such as available to builders for similar purposes.

Light stains will be removed by a solution of oxalic acid, as used on stains in wood. Application of a 'poultice' made from kaolin and benzine will remove grease marks.

White marble may be bleached back by use of most household bleaches or by an application of diluted hydrogen peroxide and ammonia mixture—but do this outside as the fumes are dangerous.

Rough surfaces can be buffed down with pumice powder, fine carburundum or any other fine abrasive and finished off with kaolin or French chalk. Finally washed down with soapy water and polished with any clear furniture polish.

Cracks, holes, etc., can be repaired by filling with epoxy resins (such as Araldite) mixed with appropriate powder colours to match the marble.

Mirrors

There comes a stage when old mirrors cease to perform any useful function and need resilvering. It is of course the old glass that should be preserved and any good glass merchant will resilver a mirror with an antique finish, so that it does not look too brash and new. Before you have any mirror resilvered, however, take advice from a reputable dealer as you can easily reduce the value of a good mirror by resilvering. A compromise is to remove the old glass and replace it with a new mirror, keeping the old glass carefully for replacement when required.

Mirrors can be preserved by carefully dusting off the reverse side and resealing with a brush coat of clear French polish or polyurethane varnish.

Ormolu

Embellishments of ormolu are brass or bronze castings which have been gold plated by a process of dissolving gold in mercury and then driving off the mercury by heating, leaving a deposit of gold on the surface. This process is highly dangerous and no longer practised. Electro-plating with gold can be undertaken by some platers, but is not recommended.

The best methods of 'brightening up' ormolu are as follows:

Remove the mounts and clean off the worst of the dirt with a wire brush. Now immerse completely in ammonia solution and work over the surfaces with a soft brush. Leave in the solution for 10–15 minutes and on removal plunge *immediately* into a bath of water.

If the condition of the mountings is very bad, instead of the above, hang the pieces on wire and immerse in a solution of half nitric, half sulphuric acid. After a short immersion they will start to fizz and bubble and should be removed and rinsed in plenty of water to which an alkali, such as washing soda, has been added. Dry off with a soft rag and you will find the surfaces have been slightly etched and are matte. The highlights should now be brought up with a steel burnisher. An old chain burnisher is the best thing to use. You can obtain them from: T. Marten & Son Ltd., Bridgeman Street, Walsall, Staffs.

Otherwise you can use any bright steel tool, such as the back of a small gouge or a bright hard steel rod. This treatment will produce a bright finish contrasting with the matte surfaces. Finally the pieces can be wax polished, or if you prefer, coated with a suitable lacquer.

Papier Mâché

Papier Mâché furniture and trays, usually inlaid with Mother of Pearl designs and decorated with paints, were popular during Victorian times and are now regaining their former popularity.

Missing pieces of Mother of Pearl can be glued back into place with epoxy resin glues. New pieces of Mother of Pearl can be worked to shape on a grindstone. Missing or broken areas of the papier mâché/lacquer finish can be filled with epoxy resin fillers such as plastic padding, rubbed down smooth with fine sandpaper; brush coated with black satin or ebonised French polish and then coated with a clear polyurethane lacquer.

Rush Seats

As with cane seats, it is not easy to find anyone who will do rushing. The technique is not, however, hard to acquire. If you know a friendly handicraft teacher or occupational therapist, they will show you how it is done in a short lesson. There are several alternatives to rushes which can be obtained from handicraft shops, as can books giving detailed instructions. If you have difficulty in finding supplies try Dryad Ltd., Northgates, Leicester, who specialise in all types of handicraft materials.

Turning

Small articles, such as knobs, finials, pillars, legs, etc., can be turned quite satisfactorily on a do-it-yourself lathe driven by an electric drill. These lathes are relatively inexpensive. The only other tools you need are a few turning chisels. Several good instruction books on turning are available, such as *Woodturning* by P. Blandford; *Woodturning* by Geoff Peters and *Practical Wood Turner* by Frederick Pain—all are available from Stobart & Son Ltd., 67/73 Worship Street, London E.C.2, or from booksellers.

Upholstery

When working on upholstered furniture care must be taken to protect the material from soiling with stains, polishes, strippers, and such like. It is therefore prudent to cover all upholstery before starting work with plastic sheeting, carefully held in position with self adhesive tape of the kind used by motor body repairers. A few minutes spent on these simple precautions will save endless time and provide adequate protection to vulnerable areas.

The renewal of upholstery is a separate craft, but simple tasks, such as rewebbing, recovering and restuffing chair seats present no great problems to the average handyman or woman.

The tools required are as follows:

A webbing stretcher which can be made from a spare piece of $\frac{3}{4}''$ to $1''$ board.

A magnetised upholsterer's tack hammer.

A cranked upholsterer's ripping chisel for knocking out old tacks.

A straight and a curved upholster's needle.

Twine and webbing.

A tacking stapler is also a great time saver and a useful, though not essential tool.

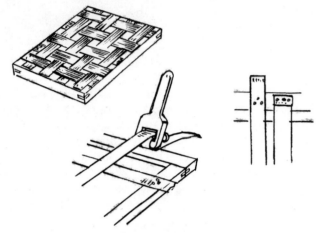

A. *Woven webbing seat.*
B. *Tool for stretching webbing.*
C. *Method of securing webbing with cut tacks.*

If the webbing is sound and the stuffing even on a piece of upholstered furniture, you need do no more than replace the top cover. Beneath the cover you will find a layer of either hessian or white cotton material holding the stuffing in place. The first step is to remove as much of the accumulated dust and dirt as possible by a combination of vacuuming and beating.

It is then easy enough to cut a piece of the new covering material roughly to size and shape. Start at the front edge and turn in about half to three quarters of an inch of material and tack it into place with cut tacks of suitable size. Do not stretch the material too much. Secure it at one end first, and then at the other end before securing the rest of the length with additional tacks.

Now carefully fold in the corners snipping the selvage where necessary with a pair of scissors to ensure that the corners are neat and do not show any unsightly lumps. Next secure the material along the back edge, straining the material very slightly. This time place the first nail in the centre of the back, but do not drive it home in case it needs readjustment. Now nail the two ends down, ensuring that the material is perfectly flat. Next secure the two sides similarly.

On occasion it will be found that the stuffing has become compressed or displaced and a re-arrangement of the horse hair, or cotton waste, is required. It may also be sensible to increase the thickness of the stuffing and the judicious use of latex foam, such as Dunlopillo, is the most satisfactory way of providing extra cushioning. Care must of course be taken to ensure that the final surface is smooth and free from lumps.

When the webbing is either broken or stretched to such an extent that the bottom of the seat sags, the entire webbing base must be replaced with new material. All of the old tacks must be removed and new webbing stretched over the frame by first securing one end to the frame with stout cut tacks. Leave a couple of inches of the webbing free and nail it down with three or four tacks. Now fold the spare length over the already nailed area and secure again with another row of tacks. Now, using your stretching tool, strain the webbing on to the opposite rail as tight as you can pull it and nail down in a similar manner. Next comes the stuffing and on top of that the hessian under cover.

When dealing with sprung seats, a webbing base has first to be nailed into place. The coil 'hour glass' springs are now sewn into place with twine, using the curved upholsterer's needle. Each spring needs to be held down by four loops of twine so that it cannot move from its correct position. Next the springs are compressed by threading and looping more twine through the top rings of the springs. A length of twine is secured by a tack to the frame and threaded over the top of the row of springs, each spring being secured in place with a slip knot. The springs at the edges of the seat being compressed much more than those in the middle so that the chair begins to assume its final shape. Next comes a layer of hessian to cover the springs then a layer of stuffing or latex foam and lastly the under cover.

When the top cover has been tacked into place, the edges should be covered with a gimp or braid. This is both glued into place with rubber adhesive and secured with gimp pins, which have small unobtrusive heads which bury themselves in the braid.

If you want to go more deeply into the craft of upholstery the following books are recommended: *Upholstery* by Malcolm Flitman and *Practical Upholstery* by C. Howes.

Warped Boards

One of the most difficult problems frequently encountered is that of warped wood in tables, bureaux fronts and the like. This happens because the moisture content of the wood changes due to the conditions in which the piece of furniture is kept—central heating is the greatest cause.

Although steaming and wetting will produce a temporary cure and boards may be straightened by cramping flat, unfortunately they will return to their twisted shape, so all the effort will have been in vain. However there are certain occasions when remedial measures of a permanent nature can be applied.

In cases where a table top has warped and pulled away from its frame, it will often be found that the top was secured with either glue blocks or insufficient screws driven in at an angle through the supporting frame. In most cases the board can be pulled back into true by blocks held to the frame in a groove. In this way the screws can be driven home straight into the wood, and will be much more secure and will not be able to bend.

Some flat tops, particularly of centre pillar tea tables, can be held flat by screwing a number of stout supports to the underside where they do not show.

Yet a third method is to take a rebate out of the underside

of the edge of the warped top to about half the thickness and to screw and glue in a stout piece of wood with the grain running longways thus making the offending board conform to its required shape.

This technique is useful when dealing with warped bookcase door frames. In order to straighten up a badly bowed frame it may be necessary to remove up to three-quarters of the thickness of the bowed member of the frame to make it sufficiently pliable to be pulled back into shape. Instead of using hardwood for straightening a piece of multiply marine plywood may be used, as this is less liable to distortion than ordinary timber. Glueing and cramping should be enough to hold the frame flat and avoid the use of unsightly screws in a situation where there is insufficient wood remaining to allow them enough depth to hold firm.

Appendix

RESTORERS' DIRECTORY

Always look in your local "Yellow Pages"
for possible sources of supply

Barometer Parts & Repairs
Garner & Marney Ltd
41 Southgate Road
London N1

Brass Casting
John Lawrence & Co (Dover) Ltd
Granville Street
Dover

Escare Metal Co Ltd
195 Bexhill Road
St. Leonards-On-Sea

Brass Handles and Fittings
J. D. Beardmore & Co Ltd
1–3 Percy Street
London W1

Period Furniture Hardware Co Inc
123 Charles Street
Boston Mass 02114
United States

John Lawrence & Co (Dover) Ltd
Granville Street
Dover

H E Saville Ltd
365 Filey Road
Southport

Brass Inlay—Strip Sheet
Smith & Son Ltd
42–52 St John Square
Clerkenwell
London EC1

Cane & Rush Seats
Wycombe Cane & Rush Weavers
Ltd
Victoria Street
High Wycombe

Carving Tools—Chisels
Ashley Iles (Edge Tools) Ltd
East Kirkby
Spilsbury
Lincolnshire

French Polish
Furniglass Ltd
136/8 Great North Road
Hatfield
Herts

French Polish Supplies
Gedge & Co Ltd
68 John Street
London EC1

Golden Star Polish Manufacturing
Inc
400 E 10th Avenue
North Kansas City
MO 64116
United States

Mohawk Finishing Products
Company
1121 Isabel Street
Burbank
California
United States

Gold Leaf

Geo. M. Whiley Ltd
Victoria Road
South Ruislip
Middlesex

Horsehair Materials

John Boyd
Castle Cary
Somerset

Lampshades

Wray Ltd
604 Kings Road
Chelsea

Leather Tools

Taylor & Co Ltd
54 Old Street
London EC1

Mahogany

James Latham Ltd
Lee Side Wharf
London E5

Wm. Mallison & Son Ltd
130 Hackney Road
London E2

Mirrors

Semnat Glass Ltd
73 Hackney Road
London E7

Metal Polishing Materials

T A Hutchinson Ltd
16 St Johns Lane
London EC1

Musical Box Repairs

Keith Harding Ltd
93 Hounsly Road
London N7

Saw Sharpening

Columbia Saw Works
Hackney Road
London E1

Stringing

Crispin & Son Ltd
92 Antair Road
London E1

Tapestry

Arthur Lee & Son
Stanley Road
Birkenhead
Cheshire

Tortoiseshell Ivory

F Friedman Ltd
Kudu House
60 The Minories
London EC3

Table Leathers

Antique Leathers Ltd
4 Park End
South Hill Park
Pont Street
Hampstead
London NW3

Specialist Tools—Vinamould

Alex Tiranti Ltd
70 High Street
Theale
Berks

Veneers, Inlays

Crispin & Son Ltd
92 Curtain Road
London EC2

Woven Fabrics

Regina Fabrics
40–42 Great Eastern Street
London EC2

Index